TRACING THE HISTORY OF HOUSES

BILL BRECKON,
JEFFREY PARKER
& MARTIN ANDREW

With illustrations by Pip Challenger
and Trevor Yorke

First published 1991
This new edition 2000
© Bill Breckon, Jeffrey Parker & Martin Andrew 2000
Reprinted 2001

COUNTRYSIDE BOOKS
3 Catherine Road
Newbury, Berkshire

To view our complete range of books,
please visit us at
www.countrysidebooks.co.uk

ISBN 1 85306 644 3

Designed by Graham Whiteman

Produced through MRM Associates Ltd., Reading
Printed by J.W. Arrowsmith Ltd., Bristol

Contents

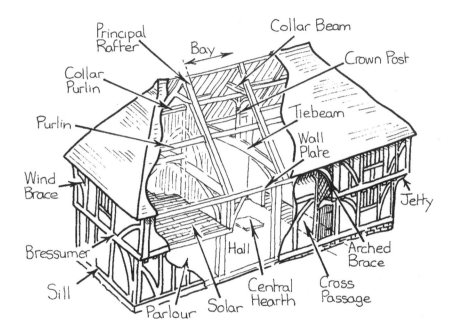

Timber-frame house details

INTRODUCTION

England's architectural past is a particularly rich one and some of the finest old buildings in the world are to be found here: great palaces, imposing country houses, inspiring cathedrals and monumental public buildings.

But our architectural heritage extends far beyond the mere expression of pomp and power by Church and State, or a reflection of private affluence and civic pride. For in almost every town and village, and around every other corner in the countryside, there are further evocations of earlier times and of the people who lived in them. Not the rich and the famous, but rather the ordinary citizens – the farmer and the clerk, the craftsman and the merchant – living in their everyday houses.

These Englishmen's homes are still to be seen everywhere, some plain and simple, others elegantly appointed and elaborately decorated. Mellow medieval timbers for example remind us of the richness of the wool trade, sweeping Georgian terraces the beginnings of the Empire. In the countryside a village row of cottages may reflect the changing fortunes of agriculture while in the town villas and terraced housing plot the progress of the Industrial Revolution.

The five sections of the book have different uses. The first puts the everyday house in historical context, charting the social, economic and political pressures that all contributed to making our old houses the way they are.

Since geography has also shaped our houses, Section Two gives information about the regional variations in building styles and materials – from the mud cob cottages of Devon to the fortified tower houses of the northern border country.

Section Three will help those who want to make a more detailed study of the basic components of a house. There is a wealth of information about the roof and the walls, about windows and doors and about floors, staircases, fireplaces and chimneys. Each chapter may be read right through, or the cross references from the previous sections can be used to identify passages of interest.

Section Four is intended mainly for those who live in older houses as it contains hints on repair, restoration and replacement. Owners of old houses should be aware that there are sometimes restrictions on what alterations can be undertaken. Restrictions apply for instance if a house is a Listed Building or if it lies in a Conservation Area.

Section Five will be particularly useful when you are out and about, enabling you to identify and date, with a fair degree of accuracy, the houses you come across in your travels. By answering some simple questions about the house in front of you, you will be able to 'home in' on its style, type and age. Houses very often do not remain in their original condition: they are altered, enlarged, improved, renovated, so that their outside appearance might well conceal a very different heart within. Only inside investigation or local records enquiries will reveal everything. Nonetheless this section will enable you to identify fairly precisely the face that a house shows to the world.

The houses around us are both a legacy of our past and a monument to our increasing technological knowledge which has enabled us to use new materials and more sophisticated building methods to improve our domestic environment. The study of old houses gives an exciting insight into the practical repercussions of economic and social change; detailed knowledge of these structural developments gives a new dimension to our study of social and local history.

However you use this book, whether as a 'house-spotting' guide or a more detailed essay in history and building technique, we hope you will find, as we have, that the more you know about the everyday English house, the more you'll enjoy everyday England – in the country, in the villages and in the towns.

The text of this second edition has been fully revised and updated by Martin Andrew and many new or replacement illustrations added by Trevor Yorke, to supplement those by Pip Challenger. We hope you enjoy this new edition and continue to use it to trace the history of houses, whether your own, those around you or those in areas you visit.

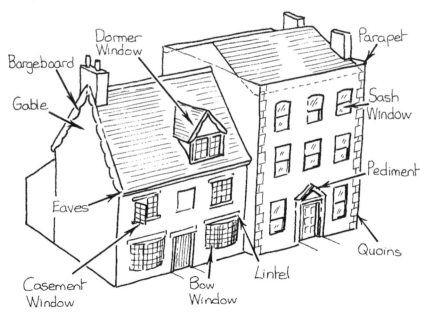

Features in a brick and stone town house

∽ I ∽

THE HOUSE
IN HISTORY

THE AISLED HALL *was developed by Anglo-Saxon craftsmen and was to form the basis of all the designs most commonly used for house building right through the Middle Ages. Later refinements included a raised dais for comfort above the earth floor and the partitioning of the end bay into areas of privacy, usually for the most important members of the household.*

The Saxon and Medieval Periods

Our earliest ancestors were nomadic hunters and, as such, did not build houses of a permanent nature. Later, the domestication of animals and the cultivation of crops led to a more settled existence and more permanent dwellings, often circular with tall conical thatched roofs. A whole family would live in the large space, with the fire smoke working its way out through a hole in the roof. Reconstructions of these houses can be seen at museums such as the Chiltern Open Air Museum in Buckinghamshire. They were grouped in villages, hamlets and farmsteads, often within defensive stockades or fences.

When the Romans invaded Britain in AD 43 they brought more advanced techniques in house building and town planning. The influence of these techniques affected the development of the local population's dwellings too, whether in existing or new towns or in the countryside. Many a wealthy Iron Age farmstead eventually replaced its circular thatched timber house with a modern rectangular villa as the focus, first perhaps in timber, then in brick or stone with tiled roofs and probably centrally heated by hot air ducts below the floor and even with a range of bath houses.

▦ TIMBER HOUSES ▦

After the gradual breakdown of Roman organization came the emergence of a recognisable Anglo-Saxon civilization. The Saxons were skilled timber workers, having built the sturdy longships that brought them to raid and ultimately to conquer England. They could square off large timber beams and fix them firmly together with mortice and tenon joints secured with wooden pegs. However for peasant housing, workshops and the like halved joints and tusked tenons were more usual, the latter being where the tenon goes all the way through the timber before being pegged. The Anglo-Saxon buildings which best show their skills were the great royal or aristocratic 'aisled hall' houses, a design which, with variations, was to be used right through the Middle Ages. By the 10th century it was said that England's wooden halls had no rivals anywhere in Europe – making everyday living fairly comfortable for the rich and privileged.

The aisled hall is basically a series of bays, rectangular boxes of timber on which the rafters lean. The excavated halls at Old Yeavering and near Cheddar were the largest timber buildings in a complex whose subsidiary buildings at Cheddar included a bakehouse, a possible ladies' bower, a cornmill and a private chapel, the latter built in stone. The side walls of the earlier halls appear to have been slightly bowed in plan (an echo of shipbuilding skills?) with the timber uprights for the walls set in a continuous trench; later the upright timbers were jointed into horizontal timbers – ground sills or sole plates – set in a sleeper trench in the ground. Not only did this add strength to the structure by spreading the loads, it also helped to prevent damage from rising damp, since posts planted straight into the ground tended to rot more quickly as water seeped easily into the end grain. The gable end walls may well have been full height, made either of timber or filled with panels of wattle and daub, or, alternatively, lower walls may have supported a hipped roof. Inside, where twin rows of wooden pillars or aisle posts divided the living space into aisles, there would have been a fire in a central hearth, the smoke from which escaped through holes in the thatched roof. This hall was the focal point for daily life where the whole household and its servants and retainers congregated, ate and slept.

Although a considerable advance in house design, the early Saxon hall was still a relatively low and sprawling construction. As the centuries progressed, however, it evolved into a more finely proportioned building in which a number of refinements added to the comfort of the occupants. It became the practice, for instance, to build at the 'upper' end of the hall, well away from the entrance doors, a raised, paved dais or platform above the rush-strewn earthen floor, and to partition off the end bay into private space for the owner and his family away from the bustle of the retainers who lived and slept on the hall floor.

By the 11th and 12th centuries the hall was often extended or adapted to provide two storerooms at the 'lower' end – the pantry for bread (from the French *paneterie* or bread store) and other dry goods, and the buttery for drink (wine and ale in butts, from the French *boutellerie* or butt and bottle store). These were often divided by a central passage running to a separate kitchen where the cooking could be done without the very real risk of burning down the hall. In many houses lower down the social scale cooking was still done over the open fire in the hall.

STONE HOUSES

While timber houses of varying quality and permanence of construction formed the basis for the vast majority of English houses, by the end of the 12th century a privileged few were able to have their homes built in stone. Stone building had at first been virtually the prerogative of the powerful leaders of church and state, and before 1100 almost the only stone buildings of note were the fortified residences of feudal overlords or the monasteries, religious foundations and churches built for rich and influential ecclesiastical authorities.

During the 12th century, though, the first great phase of church, monastic and castle building had slowed and some masons were released to sell their skills to others able to afford them.

While virtually no timber building from this period survives, a fair number of stone-built private houses do, due partly of course to the greater durability of stone. They are traditionally known as King John's Houses, since many originated in his reign. By modern standards they are by no means imposing, seldom bigger than 20 ft wide and 40 ft long, but with their two storeys and their solid stone walls, they were the envy of their day.

Many were the town houses of rich merchants, while others, built in the country, were probably attached to or near a timber hall. Living accommodation was on the upper floor – known as the hall or solar – which was usually stone

The Normans brought new stone building techniques to England and by the end of the 12th century some rich and influential citizens had their homes built of stone. A few still survive today and are generally known as King John's Houses as many of them were built in his reign.

11

paved, supported on stone vaulting carried on stone columns from the floor below. The ground storey or undercroft was used for storage, occasionally as stables and in towns for shops or workshops entered from the street. Often for security it was only accessible from above by an internal staircase. The upper storey was reached from the outside by a flight of stone steps. The best examples in the countryside include Boothby Pagnell Manor House in Lincolnshire, and for towns the so-called Jew's House in Lincoln, all of the late 12th century.

Another form of upper floor living was the tower house, where again, the main living area was on the first floor, with further private rooms on upper floors. A spiral staircase, sometimes built within the thick stone walls, sometimes contained in a projecting turret, linked the storeys. Again the ground floor was used for storage.

▦ PEASANT HOUSES ▦

Upper floor houses and aisled halls, however, were very much the exception, not the rule. For most people in the 12th and 13th centuries – and for the poorest, for labourer and peasant well into the 16th century – home remained a much cruder timber house often of poles rather than squared timber, lashed together rather than jointed, with roofs thatched with turf, heather, bracken, straw or anything else to hand. Excavation has shown that these one room or one and a half room houses were rebuilt every thirty to forty years all over an occupant's plot, and none survive. In stone areas, such as the flinty South Downs of Sussex, peasant cottages had field flint walls bound together with clay, a reconstruction of which can be seen at the Weald and Downland Open Air Museum at Singleton, north of Chichester.

The Iron Age round-house style passed rapidly out of use during Anglo-Saxon times to be replaced by the rectangular plan, with rafters lashed to a ridge pole. Low walls were often built in turf, stone or timber and the simplest would be just one room, with a central hearth, no windows, and the smoke escaping through a hole in the roof or gable. Some had a smaller partitioned space at one end, either for the cooking fire or sleeping, an echo of the grander hall and solar of their betters, but on a pitiful scale. In parts of the country the family and their animals shared the house at night.

This type continued into the Tudor age but above the poorest levels two solutions evolved to the restrictions imposed by these basic structures, that gave ordinary houses the outline that we would recognise today. They are the cruck frame and the box or timber frame.

Cruck building is an ancient building technique. Crucks, pairs of curved oak timbers set some 16 feet apart were baulked and jointed to make an arch which formed the main supports of the roof. The crucks were strengthened with the beams, joined with purlins, and for greater stability a collar beam was usually inserted a few feet from the apex. Cruck houses usually had walls of wattle and daub panels or cob. In the 15th and 16th centuries the introduction of brick or stone chimney stacks enabled the upper part to be floored over to create an upper storey.

▦ CRUCKS ▦

Crucks are large pairs of curved or angled timber baulks meeting at their tops to form a rough arch. Each pair was normally formed by halving a suitable tree so they are often symmetrical. The word 'cruck' has a similar origin to 'crutch', 'crotch' or the shepherd's 'crook'. By using pairs of crucks as the main support of the roof, the interior of the house is opened up. No longer is it all sloping ceiling: instead an open arched cross-section replaces the cramped triangular one.

Cruck building is an ancient technique but seems to have become popular in

13

England from the 12th century and continued in use in more backward parts of England into the 18th century. Its origins are obscure and much disputed but its spread into smaller houses seems to have come from its use in large hall and manor houses where crucks enabled the obstruction of the aisle post to be removed. These are the type known as 'base crucks' which are found mainly in the more prosperous south and east of England from the 12th to the 14th centuries. Oddly, the ordinary crucks which appear to have developed from the base cruck have a curious distribution in large and small houses alike which has long fascinated historians. They are to be found in Scotland and Wales but have been identified in England only to the north and west of a line running roughly from Flamborough Head to Southampton. It is uncertain why this should be so: some historians believe that cruck houses were originally constructed all over England but were replaced in eastern and south-eastern counties by more advanced building techniques. Others suggest the box or timber frame evolved in the south and east just as crucks spread down to smaller houses. Certainly there is little support for the idea that box framing spread from a cruck-free Continent as crucks occur frequently in the Netherlands, Belgium, France, particularly Brittany (a Welsh connection perhaps) and Germany.

Whatever the truth, crucks certainly proved a practical and straightforward method of constructing a house. However, they have serious limitations and effectively prevent the provision of decent upper storeys: perhaps this is why they were most popular in parts of Britain where houses remained much smaller until relatively recently.

Cruck houses were, like the hall, built in bays, each pair of curved supports being set some 12 to 16 ft apart, and the size of the house was usually defined by the number of such bays – in, for example, title deeds and building contracts. A typical cottage would be only one or two bays long while the more substantial house would have three or four bays, with the familiar domestic arrangements of central open hall section flanked at one end by the private family rooms and at the other by the pantry and buttery, often both ends with chambers over these. Walls would be made of panels of wattle and daub set in light timber-framing, cob which was popular in northern areas, or even stone in stone areas. The introduction of brick or stone chimneys in the 16th and 17th century at this social level enabled the upper part to be completely floored over. (For details of construction see p 141.)

▨ BOX OR TIMBER FRAMES ▨

In the south and east particularly, another solution to the headroom problem was emerging: that of the box frame (usually called timber frame) building. With this technique fresh skills are required to cope with the problems of

The box or timber frame construction represented an advance in house building which was developed throughout the Saxon and Norman periods. A box of solid wall timbers took the weight of the roof rafters and so the walls were not load bearing. This allowed more flexible interior arrangements and enabled the house to be built higher, with two storeys if needed.

containing the downward pressure and outward thrusts of the roof supports and covering. The roof has to be trussed, that is held or tied together by some internal arrangement of jointed timbers.

The basic module for a timber frame house is a rectangular open box of solid timbers, similar to the supporting bays of the aisled hall. However, now the rafters are supported by the wall-plate, the top beam of the side wall section, and prevented from splaying by cross timbers known as tie beams which in effect make a triangle with the rafters.

There were of course many variations of roof truss and differing regional styles which owed as much to local preference and tradition as to structural necessity.

The box frame construction had many advantages over crucks, the principal one being the possibility of piling box on box to make a building with a number of full height storeys before the roof structure need be added, indeed in towns buildings up to six storeys are found. It allowed much greater flexibility in the ground plan of a house but the need for a tie beam to counteract outward pressures meant an obstruction when walls were built relatively low. One solution was to tie the roof at a higher level, usually at that of the purlins, by means of a collar beam nearer the apex, often with braces and struts added to reduce the greater spreading pressures. Some of the commoner forms of roof trusses are the crown post, king post, queen post and arch-braced collar-beam roofs, together with the hammer-beam roof, one of the great glories of medieval carpentry which allowed much wider buildings to be roofed without a forest of aisle posts. (Details are given in the chapter on Roofs p 81.)

Unlike crucks, in box frame construction storey heights and the number of storeys possible could be greatly increased. The sturdy timbers of the frame took the weight of the roof so the walling between was not load bearing, merely needed to keep the weather and thieves out. The walls consequently had lighter framing which could be filled with wattle and daub panels, brick nogging or even clay blocks. (Further details in chapter on Walls p 105.)

While the new techniques of timber construction were beginning to provide better houses for those of more modest means, major design changes were also afoot for the hall house. Here too, timber frame, and to a much lesser extent cruck, building had raised the roof and provided taller side walls. The aisle went completely during the 14th century as its low eaves precluded better lighting of the larger hall. Instead the crosswing developed, often at each end of the hall and roofed at right angles to produce an H-plan of house, with the hall the bar of the letter. These crosswings were normally two storey and provided a chamber over the pantry and buttery and a main private room or solar over the 'high' end room. Some of the surviving stone King John's Houses were additions to halls or, in some cases such as at Little Chesterford Manor House in Essex, had timber-framed halls added in the 13th century.

The family could now escape from the hurly-burly of the communal hall to their own rooms, and particularly to the solar, the upper floor of the adjoining wing. In many of these hall and crosswing houses it is clear that they were built in phases, sometimes starting with the crosswing, sometimes the hall.

These hall and crosswing houses thus have two or three separate roofs meeting, but in the south-east of England a style evolved in the 14th century that combined all these elements under a single roof. It is called a Wealden house or, more rarely, a Yeoman's house, although neither term is strictly accurate since such houses were neither invariably inhabited by yeomen nor confined to the weald of Kent and Sussex, being found as far north as Yorkshire and as far west as Devon.

▓ THE WEALDEN HOUSE ▓

The Wealden house owes its origins to the demands of a new class of Englishman emerging in the 14th century, benefiting to some extent from the

Black Death and subsequent plague epidemics which made labour scarce and partly from the extraordinary wealth of Kentish and Sussex farmers. Despite Kent having partibility of inheritance whereby an estate or farm was shared among all the sons, there was an explosion of high quality timber-framed housing which spread into Sussex and more thinly elsewhere in the south and east.

The Wealden house combined the virtues of the hall and crosswing house under a single roof, in effect a conservative response which perpetuated the roof form of the early single storey hall houses with end bays all under a single continuous roof. However, the crosswing element was incorporated within the ends where roof trusses were set parallel to the hips and the upper floors were jettied to demonstrate that the owner could afford a two storey element.

Wealden houses usually had a hipped roof of thatch or less commonly clay tiles or stone slates, although north of the River Thames gable ends are not uncommon. Generally they were well-timbered, often with wall studs placed close together. Another characteristic of the design is the arched braces that run across the front of the hall section, from the side of the upper rooms to the roof, supporting the eaves.

The rooms at one end were used for service – pantry and buttery below with a store room, or perhaps an extra bedroom above. The use of the rooms at the other end depended very much on who was living in the house, as with hall and crosswing houses: a merchant in a town could have his shop or workshop below his best chamber, for example. Originally known as the bower or more usually as a chamber, this room was eventually called the parlour, from the name given in monasteries to the room where visitors were received, where the monks could talk or 'parler'. The room above, the solar, was reserved for sleeping. Farmers on the other hand often slept in the ground floor chamber and kept their tools, cheese presses, cheeses, hams, seed corn and other valuables in the upper chamber or that over the pantry and buttery, where they were safer from theft. As with earlier hall houses, there was usually a cross-passage screening the service rooms from the hall with access from outside doors at each end. Often the cross-passage was within the service bay to avoid reducing the hall space.

Particularly fine examples of the Wealden house are The Old Shop at Bignor in Sussex, and Synards at Otham in Kent, but although the design features of such houses were fairly standard it is often difficult to recognise them. Invariably the hall has been floored over at a later date and chimney stacks added, often with jettying inserted in the hall bays to show to passers-by and neighbours that the house is now up to date and two storeyed throughout.

Other identification problems include building up or replacing ground floor walls below the jetties in brick or stone to increase ground floor accommo-

The Wealden house style emerged in the late 14th century when many farmers and merchants, newly rich from the prosperous English wool trade, built modest sized versions of the halls of the gentry. It became a standard design for two centuries most commonly found in Kent, Sussex and Surrey. It consisted of a central hall, open to the roof, flanked by end rooms on two floors, the top floor extending outward on jetties. Jettying adds an endearing quality to these houses especially as carpenters liked to show their carving skills on the exposed joist ends. Early Wealden houses were thatched. In this example, 'Synards' at Otham in Kent, the central hall has been floored over and a 17th century dormer window inserted in the new upper floor.

dation or because of decay in the original timbers. Inside, however, evidence of the earlier wall can often be found in the surviving timbers and in the mortice slots where the original studs and posts were tenoned in or by the cut outs for the plate in the underside of the jetty beams. These will usually be a foot or more inside the line of the present ground floor wall. The unglazed mullioned windows will often have been enlarged and new windows inserted in different positions, and the outside 'look' of the house may be disguised by rendering or by tiles hung over the timbers. These additions and alterations mean that no one is really sure how many Wealden houses still remain after four to six centuries. A few are now museum pieces, having been dismantled, restored and re-erected on sites open to the public, such as Bayleaf at the Weald and Downland Open Air Museum in Sussex which even had the luxury of an upstairs privy.

The Wealden house was a relatively inflexible plan type with its single roof and, while it could be adapted internally, it could not effectively be enlarged or modified to changing house styles. It belongs fundamentally to very conservative and stable communities with sufficient wealth to produce virtually standardised comfortable houses for their strata of society. The Wealden house was never the house of the majority of the population, even in wealthy Kent. Nonetheless, the growing wealth of the country in late medieval and Tudor times led to an increasing demand for better houses and to what has been described as the Tudor building boom, which actually lasted well into the Stuart period.

The Sixteenth Century

The period from the closing years of the 15th century until the beginning of the 17th century saw increasing commercial success for England, and a substantial population explosion – from less than three million people to more than four and a half million. In fact, of course, the population in effect recovered from the economic collapse of the early 14th century, a collapse compounded by the Black Death of 1348–50 and subsequent epidemics of this devastating bubonic plague. The population increase coincided with a spectacular Tudor inflation that greatly benefited farmers and primary producers who saw their prices rise in a society based on fixed rents or commuted feudal dues. The result was surplus cash which could be invested in improving houses and what are now known as 'lifestyles'.

Small wonder that it was a boom period in house building. The newly prosperous middling classes wanted to extend their existing properties or to replace the shabbier ones. Thus homes built of, say, cob, were pulled down and spanking new houses put up, built in stout oak, in stone, or in the later 17th century, in brick which was by then coming into more plentiful supply. Many built new, but those yeomen with larger hall houses modernised and adapted: canny country men.

The 'Great Rebuilding', as it is now known, occupied a wider time span than the 16th century and took place at varying times in different regions from the mid-16th century into, in some more backward parts of the country, the early 18th century. No matter: whenever it took place it required armies of carpenters, masons, bricklayers, daubers, thatchers and tilers, all highly skilled men who had served a rigorous apprenticeship and were proud of the greater freedom and respect that their skills brought them.

Not all the houses being built, however, were of solid and superior construction. The smaller cottages built for the poorer members of the burgeoning population were more often than not flimsy affairs and just about all of those built before the 16th century have long since perished. The 16th and earlier 17th century period houses which we today call 'cottages' are invariably the former homes of the richer yeomen. In most of England (particularly in southern and central areas) these houses were built in the village. Only when the village's common fields were enclosed did it become the custom for farmers to build iso-

A typical town scene with timber-framed and jettied houses rising three storeys above a narrow lane.

lated farmhouses in the centre of their new hedged fields.

Their houses would have been looked on with envy by their poorer neighbours whose homes were often hastily erected, since a man was allowed to build on common land, provided that, starting at dawn, the house was sufficiently completed to have a fire burning in the grate at sunset. So many such hastily-erected homes were built that it caused official concern over the encroachment on common land, and in 1589 a law was passed to try and control such building. It has to be admitted, though, there was a lot of connivance. It suited the farmer to have his wage labourers living nearby, so blind eyes were turned and it became yet another law more honoured in the breach than the observance.

The swelling ranks of skilled craftsmen were nonetheless providing great numbers of well-built houses which still stand sturdily today in our country villages and towns and, to a lesser extent, in the cities (where they have been more often destroyed by fire or deliberately replaced). Most of the wealth of the country was concentrated in the south, so it is in this region that most examples survive. It was in the south too that innovations in design and building techniques generally started. They spread only slowly to the rest of the country: it could take as long as a century for new ideas fully to permeate the more isolated regions in the north. For this reason a house in the south-east of similar design and construction to one, say, in the north-west may well have been built up to a hundred years earlier.

As we have seen, the box frame was very much a southern style, while cruck frame construction was most popular in the north and west. Box frame construction, with its greater flexibility, spread slowly northwards and probably hastened the decline in cruck building, which had petered out by the end of the 18th century, the last such being the roughly built houses of the very poor in the Lake District. The box frame had also disappeared for housing in the south-east soon after 1700 but found a home in the barnyard for another century and a half.

The Fireplace and Chimney

Two closely interrelated factors significantly affected the internal arrangements of English homes in the Tudor period. One was the demise of the large open hall that had originated in medieval times. Its end was hastened by the need for more and better accommodation, providing more individual rooms within the house, and an increasing taste for privacy. The other factor was the advent of enclosed chimney stacks, replacing the open hearth.

Early attempts to overcome the problem of smoke-filled rooms, using hoods and flues of wattle and daub, had been unsatisfactory, not least because of the fire hazard. The very well off, and those fortunate to live in areas where it was readily available, could have chimneys made of stone, but these were comparatively rare, and it was not until bricks were being produced in quantity that the chimney became an integral part of ordinary homes. Its introduction meant that the upper part of the open hall was now smoke-free, so a floor could be put in, providing a two storey house.

Although brick chimneys were often installed in, or added to, outside walls, many replaced plastered timber smoke hoods and flues which had been formed over the central hearth or were built where the open fire had been. In these the brick chimney emerged through the middle of the roof. This new arrangement required more sophisticated joinery techniques to butt the upper floor around the chimney.

The need for more rooms and the introduction of the central, enclosed chimney stack meant a radical departure from the medieval concept, which had held sway for generations, of a house as a central open hall with parlour and service rooms at each end. Now the upper storey – or storeys, for the timber frame house, especially in towns, was growing ever taller – became devoted to bedrooms, a convention that remains to this day. For it was in this period that the farmer and townsman started habitually going upstairs to bed.

The central stack also meant that the back-to-back fireplace could be installed, bringing warmth to two rooms. Those on the ground floor could thus be used for the purpose that best suited the household. A common arrangement was to build the chimney in what had been the screens passage dividing the hall from the pantry and buttery. These, now heated, became new parlours, or the 'low' end changed from the medieval buttery and pantry into the kitchen with cooking on a spit in the new wide fireplace. This left the old parlour at the 'high' end unheated and it either needed an external chimney, became a summer parlour or was even relegated to a service room.

An alternative design placed the chimney stack between parlour and hall, that is at the 'high' end, with fireplaces to heat both chief rooms. Whichever the arrangement chosen, it was also found that a convenient space was created between the stack and an adjacent outside wall in which to build the staircase behind the stack. It also formed a draught lobby behind the main door when inserted in the screens passage, to produce the 'lobby entry' plan characteristic of the late 16th and 17th century farmhouse in the south and east of England.

Chimneys rapidly became status symbols, so much so that it is not uncommon to find Tudor and Stuart houses with more chimney flues than fireplaces: this was the owners showing off to their neighbours. Much skill was lavished, too, on the design and decoration of the stacks where they emerged from the roof. Among the most pleasing are those in spiralled and patterned brickwork copying gentry houses and mansions, but ribbed and keeled ones are more common. Many originals survive, although not a few were built in Victorian times, to Tudor design.

▨ Timber-frame Developments and Windows

While the bricklayers were showing off their new-found skills, the carpenters were revelling in their ancient ones, and a wealth of fine details and elaborate carving, both inside and out, was a characteristic of Tudor and Elizabethan timber buildings. This was to the evident delight of their clients who also gloried in showing off their new-found wealth and status. Consequently the carpenters were not economical in their use of wood. Much more was used than was strictly necessary for structural reasons and wood was extensively incorporated for purely decorative effect, such as in close vertical studding for the walls and in the marvellous 'magpie' work of the West Midlands and the north-west. This

Brick became a very popular home-building material during the great rebuilding of the 16th century, especially in Kent, Surrey and Sussex. The innovation of the enclosed chimney stack made it possible to have more private rooms within the building and meant a radical departure from the medieval concept of living accommodation.

elaborate form of decoration is based on a series of rectangular panels, each containing diagonal wooden strips or curved braces to form an overall geometrical pattern. The design was later heightened by blacking the timber and whitening the plaster in-fill. Fine examples are to be seen in Shropshire, Herefordshire and Cheshire with perhaps the most famous of all, Cheshire's Little Moreton Hall.

In the towns, constrained by their ancient protective walls, land for building was at a premium, and the Tudor builders tried to solve the problem, as have their 20th century successors, by building upwards. Creaking and unwieldy-looking houses soared to four, five and even six storeys. They were invariably

In timber buildings in East Anglia, and particularly in Suffolk, it became fashionable to cover both the timber and the wattle and daub panels with plaster. This was then scored and combed into decorative patterns, or moulded into shapes and designs. This technique was called pargetting (from the French par – all over, and jeter – to throw). The fashion for pargetting was at its height from the late 16th century through the 17th, and fell from favour during the mid-18th century.

25

jettied, each storey overhanging the one below. This certainly provided more space on upper floors but its popularity was more likely dictated by fashion rather than function. Those jettied Tudor mini-skyscrapers that still remain in our towns have often lurched and become deformed by time, showing how difficult it was to build high and be really secure using 'green' or unseasoned timber. Still, they have survived hundreds of years and their crookedness adds to their delight.

As well as the Great Rebuilding, the 16th century also saw much renovation and alteration: notably in the replacement of windows. Narrow unglazed medieval mullions were taken out and bigger glazed windows put in. (The process was to be repeated a couple of centuries later when the windows of many Tudor houses were replaced with Georgian ones.)

▨ Modernising the Longhouse

In the country, too, it was a time of change and reconstruction and such change would have been particularly noticeable in England's 'highland' zone of the north, West Midlands and south-west. We have seen how in the middle and south of the country the yeoman farmers usually built their homes in the village, venturing forth each day to cultivate their separate strips of arable land. The few isolated houses in this countryside would be medieval manors, extensively modernised. In the 'highland' zone, however, the 'long' house, standing on its own or in small, scattered hamlets, had been traditional for generations. It enabled those keeping livestock, to be in closer touch (and smell) with their flocks and herds. One long roof sheltered both a narrow house, one room deep, and the byre for the animals.

In this period of prosperity, however, the animals were ousted from the end of the house to separate quarters in the farmyard, and the original byre was converted to living accommodation. More often than not, with the addition of chimneys, it became a proper kitchen. Large numbers of longhouses were so converted, and they can often be recognised by differences in the basic structure at what was once the byre end, where less care was originally taken in building.

Sometimes the byre continued to be used for animals but access from the house was sealed off. Such buildings are called 'laithe' houses, from the local word for byre, and are found mostly in Yorkshire. The tradition continued into the 18th and 19th centuries, evolving into houses with barns or byres attached and under a continuous roof.

The Seventeenth and Eighteenth Centuries

The 17th and 18th centuries were to see further great changes in house design, both in town and country. In the town, a major disaster prompted legislation which was to alter the whole appearance of the urban scene: in the country a deluge of further Acts of Parliament enforced a new way of life, good for some but disastrous for many.

The look of our towns was altered by the 1666 Great Fire of London and the Building Acts that it engendered, while the shape of the countryside was transformed by the 18th century Enclosure Acts which overturned centuries-old agricultural practices.

Town Planning

For centuries kings and parliaments had issued edicts, formulated laws and drawn up regulations, all largely ignored, in attempts to minimise the ever-present risk of fire in England's crowded towns. With so much timber used in house construction and with haphazard cheek-by-jowl building, the towns were packed to their walled seams and were veritable tinder-boxes. One small spark could lead to a major conflagration. All the laws, edicts and regulations, however, had little effect, as was so dramatically demonstrated not only in London's Great Fire of 1666 but in other, earlier infernos, such as those that had gutted the centres of Bury St. Edmunds and Northampton.

The risks of fire – and disease too – were further compounded in the 17th century by a considerable increase in speculative building. Most earlier houses had been built to order, the builder's client becoming the occupier. Now the speculative builder was putting up 'off the peg' homes, for rent or lease to anyone, frequently during or after construction. Without the intimate relationship between customer and constructor it was inevitable that corners were cut and standards lowered to maximise profit. Not that all speculative housing was poor: some of the builders raised stucco or brick terraces which were more fireproof than the timber-framed houses still being built all around. Perhaps the finest was the old Covent Garden piazza of the 1630s designed by Inigo Jones for the Earl of Bedford with houses for (high) rent.

Fire was not just a London problem and although the laws enacted generally referred to the capital, they were taken up by other towns and cities. In 1605 James I had decided that action was needed and banned any fresh building in timber in London: only brick and stone were to be used. But the regulations, and other controls introduced in subsequent Building Acts, were largely ignored, such was the demand for new houses. Builders continued throughout the first half of the century erecting many cramped and unsafe houses both within and outside the city walls. London, with its population booming, infilled yards and courts and compounded the problems with chronic overcrowding, insanitary conditions and consequent disease.

The last great outburst of the bubonic plague, the infamous Black Death, in 1665 owed much to the overcrowded squalor of London. The subsequent Great Fire of London not only brought about fresh laws but also it seems, a change in attitude, for the Rebuilding Act of 1667 was for the most part observed. One undoubted factor in its success was in the tighter control of building practices on site, by official building inspectors appointed to examine the work as it progressed and make sure the minimum standards were being met.

The 1667 Act and those that followed it in the next century changed the appearance of London by law (and of other towns and cities by example and fashion) through specifying standard types of houses that could be built, and by relating the size of house to the width of the street. It is interesting that the builder of this period, no longer able to indulge private fancy in overall design, increasingly used ornamentation around doors and windows to give some stamp of individuality to his building. The 1667 Act, like earlier laws, referred specifically to London but its commonsense technical provisions and the new uniformity of style spread countrywide, adopted by many other towns and cities eager to ape the styles and fashions of the capital.

The Act laid out with a fair degree of precision four types or 'sorts' of houses that were allowed to be built. Terraced houses predominated to make the best use of limited space, and the first, and smallest, sort of house described was two storeys high, with cellar below and attic above. It was decreed that the principal rooms had to be no less than 9 ft high, and the cellar and attic at least 6 ft 6 inches. The thickness of the walls was laid down too: two bricks thick to the first floor, one-and-a-half up to attic level, one brick thick to the roof.

The shape and appearance of towns was further regulated by provisions governing the width of the streets. These 'first sort of houses' were the only ones allowed in the narrowest streets or 'by lanes', 14 ft minimum width, sufficient to allow two carts to pass each other. In broader streets, 'the streets and lanes of note', of some 18 to 24 ft, 'the second sort of house' could be built: one of three storeys with attic and cellar if desired. Again there were regulations on ceiling heights and wall thicknesses, as there were for the 'third sort of house', imposing four-storey dwellings which were to be set in the few main streets of 30 to 40 ft wide. (The 'fourth sort of house' was one 'of the greatest bigness' set in its own grounds and its size and shape were similarly regulated.)

One of the remarkable consequences of the building regulations of the latter part of the 17th century was that different social classes lived in similar types of houses, the only real difference being in size. It is true, however, that the smaller types of houses tended to be less well built than the larger ones – and in many city areas they quickly degenerated into overcrowded slums, with the sort of social life depicted in Hogarth's 'Gin Lane'.

All these rules and regulations obviously affected the outward appearance of the house, enforcing a simplicity and a symmetry unseen in the apparently higgledy-piggledy Tudor and Elizabethan town. But throughout the 17th century other influences had been at work, notably the classical ideas seeping across from post-Renaissance Europe. Particularly influential was the work of the Italian Andrea Palladio who adapted classical styles for use in domestic architecture and whose book was translated into English in 1676. The great architects of the day – such as Inigo Jones in the early part of the century and Christopher Wren in the latter half – influenced domestic architecture through others imitating the styles and details they had used in great private houses and public works.

Although architects and masons had always used drawings to show the important client their designs, Inigo Jones took the idea to new heights of technical perfection in imitation of his Italian mentors. Thus the client would know exactly what the house would look like before its construction. At the small house level a written contract would have rarely contained drawings and generally went no further than specifying the number of bays long, the storeys and the materials, as well as the price (and the amount of beer and food to be supplied to the craftsmen during building operations). Of course, from the builder's previous work the customer would know roughly what the house would look like.

Such vagueness was no longer appropriate in the 17th century where, with standardised shapes and sizes, it was the refined detail that was most important. Hence the need for drawings. Some classical details had already begun to appear in Tudor and Elizabethan times but as the 17th century progressed they were to be seen more and more, in pediments over the front door, for instance, in decorative mouldings and around the windows, and on cornices, parapets and balustrades concealing the roof, and pilasters stretching from ground to eaves level. Also influential in the overall 'look' of the house was the sash win-

The introduction of the classical style of architecture in the 17th century with its clean symmetrical lines marked a complete departure from the timber-framed houses of the previous centuries. Rows of well-proportioned windows and an imposing central front door were major design changes which were to set the pattern of house styles for the next two centuries.

dow (see chapter on Windows p 126) from the late 17th century onwards which tended to make window proportions taller and relatively narrower.

The decline of the traditional housewright, who might take six months to complete a one-off house, and the rise of the professional architect, who might produce fresh designs in as little as six days, meant that ideas were able to travel, and could be copied much more quickly. The new styles of building spread rapidly across the country. In some areas there was less change, due mainly to the intractability of some building stone and the unsuitability of cob for architectural enrichment, but everywhere at gentry level and higher the new styles were embraced, using suitable imported materials.

In the Country

While 17th century legislation created new styles for town housing, later laws of a very different nature forced substantial change in the country. Since the 15th century landowners had sought to improve their land, often clearing villages and enclosing the common fields for sheep runs. Indeed, enclosure had provoked crises and government investigations in Tudor times and the practice accelerated throughout the 17th century. However, it was the flood of 18th century Enclosure Acts that literally altered the shape of the countryside, and the farmhouses and cottages in it.

Until then the pattern of agriculture had changed little for hundreds of years and the countryside looked very different from today's patchwork of fields. Husbandmen eked out a living from their separate strips in large open fields, a piecemeal system that was far from efficient but at least gave every villager his own land, farmed in common. However, with agriculture struggling to meet the growing demand for food from the swelling population of the towns, and major improvements in farming techniques, 18th century landowners chafed to do away with the strip system and to create larger and more efficient units.

Although enclosure both by agreement and expulsion had been happening since the 15th century, the 18th century use of private Acts of Parliament completed the transformation of the English countryside, perhaps with undue haste. The increased interest in cattle-breeding and the keeping of large herds also prompted legislation to enclose land to prevent animals straying. This hedging and fencing had to be done immediately after the Enclosure award and the expense often proved beyond the pocket of many small farmers who were forced to sell out. Field and pasture were enclosed by fence, hedge and ditch, altering the look of the land and bringing about devastating social change. Loss of common grazing for his animals as much as the actual act of enclosure ruined many small husbandmen. The husbandman might have been poor, but at least he was independent, and even those hands who worked for more prosperous yeoman farmers (owning more holdings) enjoyed a close relationship with their employers, in whose houses they often ate and slept. Now the enclosures evicted many a smaller farmer to starvation, with no option but to work for the new farmers as a landless wage-labourer or to seek work in the towns. The new generation of farmers with larger domains – and greater profits – introduced new, larger-scale systems of agriculture, changing old working practices and losing in the process the old communal spirit to a much more formal boss-and-worker relationship.

The newly-rich farmer also wanted a better type of house. In most of England he had previously usually lived in a village: now he was to build a new house on his own land, dividing up his old village dwelling into cottage rows to accommodate his workers. These are some of the terraced cottages so common in our villages and they can usually be recognised by one long communal roof, with the major chimney stack of the original dwelling now accompanied by several smaller stacks from the new fireplaces put in to heat each sub-division. Interestingly, with the reduced demand for labour on today's modern, mechanised farms – and the increased demand by farmworkers for better housing – these small cottages are often no longer required and many have been converted back into a single house, reversing in the 20th century the processes of the 18th century.

Quite a few of the farmhouses whose owners had been ruined by the enclosures became alehouses, dispensing some alcoholic comfort to the rustic workers, and many a country pub owes its origins to these days. Others, along the the village street, had their parlours converted into shops.

The new houses the farmers built on their own land were much squarer in plan than the long, one-room deep village home. Those few older isolated farmhouses that remained were often completely rebuilt, or the best parts of them incorporated into the new houses, usually forming a rear kitchen wing behind the finely-proportioned rooms of the Georgian addition.

▨ GEORGIAN PERIOD ▨

The classical style of architecture had gained popularity in the 17th century and, after the Restoration of King Charles II in 1660, finally swept away the old architectural world, at least at gentry level and above. It reached its zenith in the 18th century – the Georgian period.

The 16th century classicism of Northern Europe with its elaborate strapwork and exuberant surface decoration that underlay Elizabethan and Jacobean polite architecture had already been shown a glimpse of the future by Inigo Jones and his followers who adopted the purer styles of the Italian Renaissance, particularly the cool perfection of Palladio. After the Restoration of King Charles, Dutch and later French classicism ruled the roost until the turn of the century.

In the early 18th century under Queen Anne and George I there was a spectacular 'Battle of the Styles' with the Italian Baroque classical style slugging it out toe to toe with the revived Palladian classicism of the Earl of Burlington and his circle. It was of course all political and the triumph of Palladian simplicity over Catholic Baroque, the architecture of the absolutist European monarchies, was represented as the triumph of English rationalism. By about 1720 the wonderfully monumental Baroque of buildings like Blenheim Palace was out of favour and the austere exteriors pioneered by Inigo Jones nearly a century before swept all before them.

The apparently rambling nature of earlier large country houses had given way to a much more compact and rectangular plan, and to a house with clean and symmetrical lines, especially on the facade, where rows of well-proportioned windows were balanced about an imposing front door set firmly in the centre. These well-proportioned mansions demonstrated in bricks, stone and

Early Georgian stone houses used fine ashlar stone for the window surrounds, cornices and copings with a rougher rubble stone for the main part of the walls. Often the roof was concealed behind a parapet. As in this example, blind windows were a feature, sometimes to avoid window tax, but more often built in as an integral part of the symmetrical design of the frontage. The plain glazed sash windows shown here are uncommon. The classical style of six-pane double sashes were most often used.

mortar the rational principles of reason and order that Wren, Newton and their contemporaries believed underlay every aspect of society and the world.

In the big house, the classical details used virtually at random in late Tudor times became an integral part of the design, where a rational system of classical proportions governed the size of openings, the height of storeys and everything about the building's appearance. The ornate Dutch and shaped gables of the Jacobean period disappeared and the hipped roof tended to replace the gabled one – and the roof was often hidden behind a parapet. The hall declined still further in importance, no longer being used as a living area but merely an extension of the entrance, but often none the less grand for that. The staircase, which had been earlier often tucked away, became a prominent feature, rising grandly from the entrance hall to suites of major reception rooms on the first floor, the Italian *piano nobile*. In smaller houses its emergence often ousted the single large fireplace from its central position, replacing it by smaller ones serving individual rooms.

The smaller country house, like those for the farmer, the parson and the squire, reflected the style of its imposing neighbours, notably in becoming two rooms deep, rather than one.

In this typical Georgian 'double-pile' plan the service rooms and kitchens occupied the back of the house, while the main living rooms graced the front. The bedrooms were on the first floor. The house depth did, however, create technical difficulties, for the greater span had now to be roofed over. One early solution was to construct the roof in the shape of an M, with a gutter in the central valley, or with a flat lead section between the two ridges. The heavy tiles first used required a high-pitched roof, but by 1800, with improved transportation brought about by the digging of the canals, Welsh slates began to spread throughout the country and a lower pitch became possible, in some ways the hallmark of the Regency villa. This meant that the roof could now be covered in a single span. Mansard roofs became popular at this time too, their shape allowing additional attic rooms.

In the towns, when there was space available, similar Georgian double-pile houses were built, often two and sometimes three storeys tall, with additional attic and basement. In the latter were now to be found the kitchen and the service rooms, releasing those on the ground floor for living or for business (ideal for the doctor or the local attorney).

The facade typically might have five sash windows on the upper floor or floors, and four on the ground floor, divided by the central doorway, which had a classical hood or pediment or a projecting pillared porch. The towns were becoming even more crowded, however, so double-fronted properties tended to be built more on their outskirts. Towards the centre, the lack of space and the legacy of narrow medieval building plots meant that Georgian rebuilding was usually of the terrace type, often just one room wide and two deep, with the doorway set to one side of the front windows.

Of course, Georgian development was not confined to central rebuilding or to larger homes in the suburbs. With increasing industrialisation and trade the towns were expanding fast and a prosperous middle class was also demanding homes á la mode. The speculative builder was again hard at work, buying up or leasing tracts of land (usually outside the confines of the old city walls) and laying out squares and circuses, parades and terraces of well-proportioned houses that combined to provide a harmonious whole. The spas, like Bath in the mid-18th century, and the seaside towns by the end of the century were among the leaders in such developments, but they were to be found everywhere – and most are still in use today. In fact more than a million Georgian homes, it is estimated, are still inhabited.

Brick was by now the most popular building material outside the stone areas, but the wonderful golden and buff oolitic limestones built towns from

Bath to Stamford. Timber-frame building of traditional sort continued alongside until around 1700, when it ceased to be seen and merely became the base upon which surfaces were applied, such as render, often scored to imitate stonework, or weatherboarding, which was usually painted on houses and cottages or hung with clay tiles, slates or even clay 'mathematical tiles' that mimicked brickwork.

After the 1667 Rebuilding Act described earlier, the next important Acts were the ones of 1707, which banished the timber cornices that had been one of the glories of the period from the 1660 Restoration onwards, and 1709 which recessed the window frames 4 inches behind the face of the wall. Both Acts applied only to London, of course, and were further attempts to reduce fire risks by getting rid of as much external timber as possible. Needless to say what London did today, the rest of England did tomorrow, so the timber modillion cornice and the flush framed window gradually disappeared in all new building by the 1730s. These safety measures radically changed the appearance of Georgian town houses and simplified them so the greater purity and austerity of fashionable Palladianism chimed in with the effects of the legislation.

The final act of conformity was the 1774 Building Act which, again for London, set four rigid 'Rates' for terrace housing from First Class mansions of four storeys and three bay frontages to Third Class ones of two storeys and two bays width. The other three Rates related to separate building constraints. The Act specified quality of materials, thickness of party walls and virtually every aspect of the construction: clearly an attempt to address the notorious jerry-building of earlier London speculative terraces. The consequence was a uniformity which can be monotonous – as in Georgian Dublin where the only relief is found in the spectacular variety of doorcases, which became virtually the only area where individuality of design could sneak past the regulations.

These and other new building regulations influenced the internal arrangements of houses just as comprehensively – indeed the 1774 Act set out model interior planning too, a development compounded by the numerous 18th century 'pattern books' produced by builders and designers such as Batty Langley which, copied all over England, helped spread the uniform Georgian terrace house throughout the country. Each floor usually contained two rooms, the front room running the whole width of the house while the rear one was narrower to accommodate the staircase. The passageway from the front door made the front ground floor room narrower too, so the grandest room in the house was the first floor front, and it became the principal living room, in accordance with Italian classical practice.

From the later 18th century onwards the *piano nobile* in all rates of house became adorned with cast-iron fronted balconies, earlier houses having their first floor window converted to French doors by lowering the sills, to the great

35

enhancement of the first floor reception room. In these austere days of facade conformity the balconies and their balustrades became a focal point for decoration, especially when ironwork came into plentiful supply, and they remained principal features of town houses well into the 19th century.

Such changes in fashion as there were related more to detail and decoration than to alteration in the basic structure. Styles changed slowly through the 18th century and the greater variations are to be seen in the superior town and country houses rather than in the more lowly terraces. Among the changes of note was the arrival of later 18th century Neo-Classicism in which architects and designers copied their details and forms from the remains of Ancient Rome and Greece, rather than from Renaissance Italy. This produced increasingly detailed pediments over doors and windows, more pronounced pilasters with highly-decorated capitals and the introduction of temple-like recesses, with or without accompanying statues. Windows changed subtly, too, with panes generally becoming larger and glazing bars thinner. The three-section Venetian window, with its tall, rounded central arched window also became popular.

▨ THE GOTHIC REVIVAL ▨

Despite the splendour and harmonious proportions of classical architecture, or perhaps even because of it, by the second half of the 18th century a reaction set in. There was a desire for novelty and change and a hankering for the romantic and the picturesque in both art and architecture. There was also, it seems, a need for reassurance, for some links with the past, as the Industrial Revolution brought about rapid change both to the social structure and to the landscape.

At the same time, virtually, as the cool aloof purity of the Palladian revival held sway there was a growing interest in the ruined remains of ancient abbeys and castles, often now painted by artists and visited by fashionable coach-parties, and the rich built mock ruins and follies on their estates. This interest which became more marked by the end of the century was not merely in historical architectural styles: the medieval past was seen as the cradle of our liberties, as the essence of Englishness, and to embrace this period of architecture was to make a political point. Just as earlier we saw how the Baroque became associated with the evils of Roman Catholic absolutism, so medieval English architecture, particularly the later Gothic – Perpendicular – style, was seen to reflect peculiarly English political virtues.

On a lighter note the new-style light reading, the novel, often had a medieval setting. Two notable examples were *The Old English Baron* by Clara Reeve and Horace Walpole's *The Castle of Otranto*. Inspired with an interest in medievalism, the architectural details of the 14th and 15th centuries began to be added

36

with an almost careless abandon to houses of all shapes and sizes.

Horace Walpole himself was a pioneer of the new fashion, in his small Georgian house at Strawberry Hill near Twickenham, bought in 1750. He added all sorts of medieval excrescences – towers and battlements, pointed Gothic windows and moulded Tudor chimneys. This exuberance gave its name to a new style of architecture: Strawberry Hill Gothic.

The Gothic (or Gothick – the extra 'k' of the 18th century spelling distinguishing its early phase) Revival was at this stage a sprightly and lighthearted affair, the builders competing with each other to provide medieval details for their clients. By the end of the century the style had spread into villas and cottages. The gable-end made a comeback, with bargeboards often fretted and decorated; windows were made with pointed gothic arches and tracery patterns copied in wood or leaded lights; dripstones and mock battlements could be bought 'off the shelf'. There was little regard for historical accuracy in the early period of the revival, for the builders had scant knowledge of the evolution of medieval building systems and, in the absence of masons, were quite happy to recreate mock-gothic details in wood and plaster. These were added piecemeal to conventional Georgian houses of all types, with no attempt to return to the house plan of medieval days.

Classicism was not dead, however, and a counter-attack was mounted, particularly in the introduction of true Hellenistic architectural styles, based first-hand on actual Athenian examples rather than the second-hand versions that had come from Rome, via the Renaissance and the influential designs of Palladio. Architects, such as James 'Athenian' Stuart, visited Athens and other classical sites and drew the ruins in great detail. When they returned to northern Europe they published them and the style spread rapidly. For decades there was a battle of styles, and home-buyers could look through the builders' pattern books to choose gothic or classical details as the fancy took them.

▦ REGENCY STYLES ▦

The Regency period at the end of the 18th century and the beginning of the 19th saw the addition of many curious overseas influences to the classical lines of the Georgian style. As Britain extended her interests abroad, so the early Empire-builders brought back ideas from distant Egypt, India and the Far East; ideas that architect and designer melded into the classical framework. There was a vogue for chinoiserie (both in the use of Chinese ornament inside and in sprinkling landscape parks with Chinese-style pagodas), for the odd sphinx or two sitting somewhat incongruously on pillared facades and, with shades of Mogul India, the Hindu style, whose apotheosis is the delicious Brighton

37

Pavilion of 1815–20 built for the Prince Regent himself.

Another distinctive characteristic is a lightness of touch and a delicacy of detail. Now that most large towns had at least one iron foundry, decorative iron-work was increasingly used in staircase, balcony, window embellishment and railing. The larger foundries published catalogues of the designs that they were mass-producing, in panels of standard widths to be strung together to enhance any size and shape of balcony or window. Among the best known was the Carron company of Falkirk whose work may be seen all over the country and whose 'hearts and honeysuckle' pattern was used by the Adam brothers at the Adelphi in London and much copied elsewhere.

While much of the Regency effort was directed towards superficial decoration, rather than alteration in house shape and size, this period did see the introduction of the bow window, previously largely confined to shop fronts. The bow often ran the whole height of the house and, from shallow beginnings, deepened into a well-rounded curve towards the end of the period.

The treatment of the row of terraced houses as one architectural unit reached its zenith in the Regency, in the symmetrical perfection, for instance, of John Nash's terraces around Regent's Park in London. The spas and seaside towns were booming as the fashionable sought some fresh air and 'took the waters' – salt or otherwise. Bath continued to dominate but others, such as Leamington and Cheltenham among the spas, and Sidmouth and Weymouth at the seaside, were popular too and have been left a legacy of pretty Regency houses. The larger seaside towns and inland spas such as Brighton and Cheltenham expanded with grand terraces of stucco houses and squares as palace-like as any around Regent's Park.

From the mid-18th century onwards there was a widespread use of stucco, applied over the brickwork and often coloured to resemble stone, cream being especially popular since it resembled the much desired Bath stone. Nash used it to blend his terraces into a single architectural whole and the Adam brothers favoured it too: in any case it had academic respectability from its use in the greatly-admired villas of Palladio. Their clients, and all those who wanted 'better' houses were also undoubtedly influenced by the fact that exposed brickwork was now increasingly a less prestigious material, to be seen in factories, canal bridges and humbler homes.

Stucco had a further advantage because although the Georgian and Regency house would invariably look impressive, all was not necessarily as it should have been. The building boom, and speculative development particularly, had led to a lowering of standards, particularly as many town houses were built on short leases. The demand for bricks was often met only by using those made of unsuitable clay, insufficiently fired to withstand prolonged attack by the ele-

As towns expanded during the 18th century, terraces of well-proportioned houses were built to accommodate a fast-growing population. These were often three storeyed. Door and sash window surrounds became more ornate and ironwork decorations became fashionable on balconies, as window embellishments and railings. From the mid-18th century, it became common to apply stucco over the brick construction to resemble the cream-coloured stone so fashionable in the new Spa towns like Bath.

ments. Builders also cut costs by using mortar with too little lime in it and with much of the sand replaced by dust from the road. To encourage the mortar to set, fires were sometimes lit against the walls, but even so many of them were quick to crumble. One should not exaggerate this for despite numerous instances of 'jerry-building', houses built for fifty or a hundred year leases have survived for well over two hundred years: do we expect the modern housing estate to last that long? Stucco could, and from mid-century onwards frequently did, cover such shortcomings and of course it provided some measurement of protection from wind and rain.

This chapter has taken us into the early part of the 19th century, ostensibly the subject of the next. However, architectural developments stubbornly refuse to be so neatly pigeon-holed. Even as the Prince Regent and Nash were working on the frothy extravagancies of the Brighton Pavilion, a more earnest style was emerging: the Greek Revival, whose utter academic purity and austerity diverged startlingly from the Regency style's approachability and intimacy. Similarly in the next few decades the Gothick Revival lost its innocent sense of fun (and the 'k' off the end): earnestness became the order of the day and the Decorated Gothic became the 'correct' style, based on devout study of surviving medieval building.

The Nineteenth Century

T he Gothic Revival of the second half of the 18th century was given further impetus in the 19th century by the historical novels of Sir Walter Scott, with their detailed descriptions of medieval settings. The later styles, however, were much more sombre and serious-minded than the lighthearted fun of Regency times. Now builders and architects were trying to produce historically accurate copies of medieval styles rather than merely add gothic details.

Later on half-timbering came much into favour, with the panels between the beams filled with herringbone pattern brick nogging or with ornamental plasterwork. 'Leaded lights', with hexagonal patterns and elaborate handles and catches, were turned out en masse by the iron foundries. Tile-hung facades were popular too, and chimneys were invariably tall, with twisted shafts in moulded brick.

These styles were parallel to the Gothic Revival and represent more of a Tudor/Jacobean Revival: the yeoman cottages of 'Merrie England' were much favoured by landed estates in building cottages and villages for their tenants. In those self-same villages the new church would be in a 'correct' medieval Gothic style and the gentleman's house probably in medieval Baronial or 'Tudorbethan' (a hybrid of Tudor and Jacobean country house styles). Thus a curious hierarchy for the appropriateness of architectural styles emerged with Gothic advocates such as Augustus Pugin producing tracts criticising classical styles as pagan, uncaring and cruel, the style of arrogance, and vaunting medieval styles as humane and Christian.

Not surprisingly the Gothic Revival was much in evidence in churches, where it helped to reinvigorate ancient crafts such as the making of stained glass and ornamental floor tiles. These found their way into domestic architecture – the well-endowed parson often being a promoter of the new styles in his own home – with stained glass in half-glazed doors and in bathrooms, and ornamental tiles in halls.

ARRIVAL OF THE SUBURBAN VILLA

Much of this medieval detail was also to be seen in another type of house, the suburban 'villas' being built for the growing numbers of industrialists, merchants and professional men, to reflect their social status and wealth. The term villa had earlier been applied to the finely-proportioned renaissance-style houses built by the country gentry in the 18th century, and when the grander more formal houses, clothes and manners of the 18th century gave way to a more free-and-easy style, the villa, usually two storeys with bedrooms over living rooms and service rooms in an attached wing, fitted perfectly. The cool Regency stucco house with a shallow-pitched slate roof, French doors into a trim garden or grounds and delicate sash windows to the first floor became immensely popular. A little later in the 19th century, however, the word 'villa' was being used to describe these new properties, usually built in the suburbs, within easy reach of factory, mill or office, set in their own grounds and fairly compact in plan.

Some villas were built in good-quality brick but in others inferior brick was used and the imperfections covered over with stucco, often elaborately decorated. The battle of styles continued, with Gothic and Romanesque and mock Tudor vying with the classical. By the mid 19th century there was an increasing heaviness and solidity in style, a rejection of the lightness and frivolity of the Regency, almost as if there was an unconscious realisation that there was no place for such *joie-de-vivre* in this mechanical, industrialised age. The architectural influences were now Italian, rather than classical, with elaborate moulded architraves around windows and pediments on consoles, while doorcases became more elaborate.

By mid century one result of industrialisation was the production of large sheets of glass, so that now the window space could be filled with large panes, unbroken by glazing bars, save for the horizontal bars of the sash. Inside, the fashion was for high ceilings, with moulded cornices and elaborate ceiling roses, from which, as the century progressed, were hung gasoliers, as town gas replaced oil and colza lamps for lighting. Thick wallpapers abounded, and much of the interior timber was painted in dark colours, in imitation of old and expensive woodwork. Floors, too, were of wood, covered by a thick central carpet, and mahogany rails were popular for the main staircase. The overall effect was somewhat sombre and ponderous, a style that many people nowadays see as essentially Victorian.

▨ HOUSING THE NINETEENTH CENTURY POOR ▨

The price of the rapid material progress which allowed the rich industrialist and aristocrat their unparalleled luxuries was paid by the poor. They lived in conditions little better than those of their medieval ancestors, and in the overcrowded towns especially, arguably a good deal worse.

The towns were expanding rapidly as the dispossessed and the desperate crowded in to seek work. In London, for example, the 1851 census counted a population increase of 330,000 or 17 per cent more than in 1841, and some smaller towns more than doubled their population in a decade.

The late 18th and 19th centuries saw hundreds of thousands crammed into town centres, living where they could – whole families to a room in older houses whose former occupants had left for the comforts of the suburbs; or crammed into ill-lit insanitary dwellings thrown-up by speculative builders. Around the gaunt new factories that fuelled the Industrial Revolution grew a labyrinth of mean streets, row upon row of dingy, slate-roofed back-to-backs.

An early form of cheap mass-housing was the court – a huddle of shoddy buildings grouped around a small, open central area. Nottingham was notorious for its squalid courts, while in London's Portman Square one court in the 1840s was surrounded by 26 three-storey houses in which no fewer than 914 people lived. Its only drainage was a single sewer. In the Newlands area of High Wycombe in Buckinghamshire the courts and terraces had their few privies within a couple of feet of their wells and the streams that threaded through the houses were open sewers clogged with filth.

Many of the houses in these courts were built back-to-back, that is, they shared rear external walls as well as side walls, and had no back doors. This technique was used, too, in row upon row of cheap terraces which were particularly to be seen in industrial towns from the 1830s onwards. They not only shared rear walls which, of course, prevented healthy through ventilation, they also shared privies with many families to each privy, often located close to the solitary well. Small wonder that diseases such as cholera and typhoid were rife, and death a constant companion.

But if conditions were hellish for those in the towns, for some who stayed in the country they were almost as bad. Landless itinerant farm workers and the very poorest for whom there was only sporadic casual work on the land often endured accommodation hardly better than that for the livestock. Some shared the converted longhouses abandoned for new farmhouses by their employers; others lived in hovels built of mud, all of which have since crumbled away.

Rural squalor should not be exaggerated, however. There were numerous, if grudging, systems of Parish financial help in the 18th century to replace the medieval and Tudor charities and almshouses. For most agricultural labourers work was hard and back-breaking but their living conditions were adequate and rural communities usually more harmonious (and healthy) than those found by their fellow countrymen forced to leave the land to seek work in the booming towns and cities.

Besides this there were many chinks of light in the gloomy picture of

England presented here. Many enlightened landlords had seen fit to provide decent homes for their labourers, for a variety of reasons: through philanthropy and the desire to improve the lot of their people, through improved estate management, and occasionally even in a tidying-up and landscaping exercise for their estates, demolishing old homes and building new well-planned villages. Such schemes included early examples such as Nuneham Courtney in Oxfordshire and Milton Abbas in Dorset, both built in the second half of the 18th century, but in the 19th century the list of 'improving' landlords is prodigiously long: the Devonshires at Chatsworth, the Rothschilds in Buckinghamshire, the Dukes of Bedford in Bedfordshire and Buckinghamshire, and Lord Wolverton at Iwerne Minster in Dorset are just a few. These estate villages were paternalistic but none the worse for that and usually the owner provided schools, village halls and even pubs.

Some enlightened industrialists, too, had earlier provided better homes for their workers, notably the Strutt family in Derbyshire, who, again in the late 18th century, built solid stone houses at Belper and at Milford for the workers in their cotton mills. There were to be further such developments as the 19th century progressed but even so for the millions of factory workers packed into the towns, dirt, squalor, disease and early death were to remain the norm for most of the century.

Many of the better-off largely ignored, or were seemingly unaware of, the problems of the poor. It was not until mid-century that the national conscience was properly roused, through the exposures by such writers as Dickens and the activities of campaigning reformers, like Octavia Hill. The upright were just as appalled at the immorality of the masses, which they believed stemmed mainly from the dreadful conditions in which they were forced to live. Respectable Victorians were becoming worried too about disease: human waste often seeped into and polluted the water supplies and cholera and typhoid were no respecters of social status, a fact that became conspicuous when Prince Albert died of typhoid in 1861.

Much of the early work to provide better housing was undertaken by charitable trusts, such as the Metropolitan Association for Improving the Dwellings of the Poor, which built the first block of family dwellings in Stepney in 1849 and for which the Prince Consort himself had helped design a model tenement block. Another notable name was George Peabody, an American who had settled in London and who gave half a million pounds to raise the blocks of Peabody Buildings, many of which still stand today. Such 'flats' – the idea was imported from the Continent – made tenement dwelling more respectable, and although today we may regard the blocks as grim and stark they were vast improvements on the slums they replaced.

▧ BUILDING LAWS ▧

The legislators were busy too, spurred on by each outbreak of cholera (which *The Times* called 'the best of all sanitary reformers') and forcibly reminded of the problems by the stench of the nearby Thames – by the 1850s a putrid open sewer – which seeped into the new Houses of Parliament. So, in contrast to the building laws of the 17th and 18th centuries, which had concentrated on fire prevention and soundness of structure, those of the 19th were more concerned with health and sanitation. A series of public health and building Acts between 1848 and 1890 laid down requirements for drainage, waste disposal, refuse collection and water supply. Further, the Victorian legislators strengthened the powers and widened the responsibilities of the local authorities, most of which had been ill-equipped to deal with the overwhelming increase in their populations and the disastrous living conditions this had created.

Local councils became directly responsible for public works of drainage and sanitation, and were empowered to raise money to acquire land, clear slums and build houses. Thus was born the era of council housing, a system which through most of the 20th century provided housing for a substantial proportion of the population, until the advent of the 'right to buy' scheme and owner occupation during the 1980s.

London had made an early start in slum clearance, destroying what has been called 'the disreputable and unsavoury rookery known as Porridge Island' between St. Martin's-in-the-Fields and Whitehall, and laying out Trafalgar Square (in which Nelson's Column was erected in 1843). During the latter half of the century more such clearances were undertaken in many towns and cities. The 1890 Housing of the Working Classes Act added impetus to the policy of demolition and rebuilding by making loans available to local authorities. By the First World War, the very worst of the problems had been dealt with, although hundreds of thousands of houses and tenements, cramped and crowded and with inadequate lavatories and washing facilities, still existed. It has to be said that in many local authority schemes the new houses were not as substantial an improvement as they might have been and many of the new buildings were themselves to be condemned as slums later in the 20th century.

Victorian legislation brought fresh controls to the private sector, too, giving local authorities power to compel owners to make good unsound and insanitary property and also insisting, under local by-laws (originally the 10th century Anglo-Danish words for 'town law'), on minimum sizes and standards for new housing. Private builders contributed to the Victorian rebuilding under strict controls. Hundreds of thousands of terraced 'by-law' houses were built in the late 19th and early 20th centuries: sturdy little homes, 'two up and two down', with, if you were lucky, a kitchen at the rear and, if you were luckier still, a bathroom. Many thousands still stand and, if well modernised, continue to provide cosy and comfortable homes; others fell victim to the World War II bombs, or the bulldozer to be replaced by the dubious advantages of the high-rise flats of the 1960s, themselves progressively being demolished.

▨ HOUSING THE NEW MIDDLE CLASS ▨

The poor who suffered and the rich who enjoyed unprecedented material well-being were not the only two levels of Victorian society. There was a growing middle class of office workers, managers, shop-keepers, craftsmen and the like

While the rich Victorian favoured villas, and the poor were often housed in inferior back-to-back houses, the emerging middle classes of Victorian England discovered the suburbs. For them developers of the day built superior terraces with gardens back and front and a room for a servant in the attic area. These houses were invariably brick-built with slate roofs, but architectural embellishments differed.

– respectable, hardworking and ambitious. It was they who, searching for somewhere more pleasant to live, with more space and fresher air, spurred on the development of the suburbs and heralded the age of the commuter. Their escape from the town and city centres was made possible by the development of the suburban railway system and by the tram and the omnibus.

Many lived in superior terraces, bigger and better than the squalid back-to-backs, often with a small front patch and a larger garden at the rear. A typical better-class terrace house had a narrow hall – uncompromisingly usually called a passage in northern England. Boxed-in stairs led to a narrow landing off which opened two bedrooms. Often a further staircase led to a single attic room lit by skylights. Of the two ground floor rooms the rear was the living room (with a kitchen beyond), while the front room, or parlour, was kept for best. Others living in the suburbs were able to proclaim a greater status by living in a 'villa', not now standing alone but semi-detached.

Whether catering for the villa owner – detached or semi-detached – or for the buyer of the superior terrace, the builder was able to offer housing in a variety of styles and treatments. Almost invariably brick-built and slate-roofed, Victorian houses came with all manner of embellishments in various styles: classical, Romanesque or Gothic. Windows and doorways would be picked out with rendered pillars, lintels and arches, often with a keystone decorated with heads of historical personalities or mythical ones, or with their surrounds in different coloured brickwork. Those palely reflecting the classical style would often have a flat lintel instead of the triangular pediment favoured by the Georgians. Details tended to be a coarser and plainer imitation of the current vogue in larger houses.

For the better off, the ornate – even overpowering – Gothic style was still much in evidence. The combination of tall arched windows, often set in dark-red or greyish brick, under slate roofs of deep and varying pitches, imparted a sense almost of foreboding and this outside impression was matched by the sombre decoration inside: dark paints and papers and solid furniture. Many examples of these Gothic houses are to be found in north Oxford or in the North London suburbs of Hampstead and Highgate, previously outlying villages but swallowed up in London's sprawling expansion.

The bay window continued to be popular in all sizes of house, but instead of having a Georgian or Regency curve, it now became three sided. The ground floor bay window often had its own slate roof, or it might continue into a first-floor bay, again topped with an individual roof.

The Victorian suburban medium-size house accurately sums up the aspirations of the age, and especially of the middle class. It is increasingly solid and respectable, and shuns external flamboyance. It also reflects a growing unifor-

47

mity, a lack of individuality, which the industrial age produced. Vastly improved transport systems, and factory-produced materials available from one end of the country to the other, meant that a Victorian house in Cumberland, say, would be much the same as one in Cornwall, a different-coloured brick, perhaps, providing the only variety.

▩ THE VERNACULAR REVIVAL ▩

Mass production also brought about a decline in local skills and craftsmanship which wilted under the competition from often inferior but invariably cheaper factory-made materials. Towards the end of the century there was a reaction to this, in the Arts and Crafts Movement and in the Vernacular Revival. The former, inspired by William Morris, demanded a return to honest craft, not only in the fabric and furniture for which it is most renowned, but also in architecture. The latter expressed a reaction against both the foreign formality of the Renaissance and the excesses of Gothicism. Both movements mirrored a similar reaction in the world of painting: that of the pre-Raphaelites with whom William Morris was in any case associated.

These influences showed themselves in a brief return to the home grown English styles of the Middle Ages and the ideas were particularly taken up by the new breed of wealthy businessmen and industrialists (and their wives) who wanted houses built in the country where they could enjoy comfortably the fruits of their commercial enterprise as if to the manner – if not to the manor – born. The result was a peppering of the countryside with two types of revival house: the well-crafted, well-mannered and beautifully executed ones designed by such architects as Norman Shaw, Edwin Lutyens, Philip Webb and Baillie-Scott, on the one hand; and on the other a welter of mock-Tudor and other reproduction houses, many of great vulgarity and ostentation. Made for the *nouveaux-riches*, many were often entirely fanciful, while others sought to echo the styles of local houses centuries old. Some architects even produced houses with built-in instant aging, with sagging roofs and apparent repairs, such as added and unnecessary buttresses to support walls. Mullioned windows, leaded lights and exposed timbers were again much in evidence, and although the overall effect in many such houses is pleasing enough, in others the combination in a single building of features from several distinct periods produces an architectural hotch-potch which verges on the grotesque: it all depended on the taste of the owner and the quality of his architect, much as today.

The Twentieth Century

ollowing the First World War there were few who could continue to have built, or to run, large and purpose-built houses and country houses (although architects like Edwin Lutyens were able to provide them for those who could) and the Vernacular Revival can really be counted the last full flowering of an individualistic building style in Britain. Its influence, however, has lingered on, notably in the still popular so-called 'cottage style' and in the 'stockbroker Tudor' residences built between the wars in the outer suburbs and the dormitory towns that surround our big cities.

Other late-19th century ideas continued to influence the 20th although their ideals have often been diluted, if not swamped, by demand for mass housing and the constraints of economics. In 1898, for instance, Ebenezer Howard published *Tomorrow*, promoting the concept of a 'garden city', in which the layout and the setting of large numbers of houses were as important as their individual style. In his scheme of things the city of the future would be a carefully integrated mixture of industrial development and housing, surrounded by a green cordon of farmland, the whole a pleasant and healthy place to live and work. This is of course the ideal of most town dwellers, it would seem, and the exodus from the city centre to the suburbs and then to the villages beyond, aided by the motor car, has been one of the phenomena of our age, swamping rural villages with encircling estates of developer houses and pricing out the natives from the older cottages.

Such large-scale planning as discussed by Ebenezer Howard had previously been given little serious consideration, but the success of the first garden cities – like Letchworth (started in 1903) and Welwyn (started 1920) – and of 'garden suburbs', like that of Bedford Park in West London (designed in 1876) and Hampstead (opened in 1907), helped to foster the concept of 'new towns' in which municipal responsibilities shifted far beyond merely providing new homes for the under privileged to designing whole new communities. The New Towns Act of 1946 was a further manifestation of this well-meaning urge, although its products such as Stevenage and Harlow new towns have created their own problems.

One of the most poignant lessons of the 20th century has been that mass provision of housing cannot realistically translate the rural and romantic idylls into the products of the volume house builder. There is a fundamental problem in providing a house that appears to be hand crafted yet is built in hundreds in identical styles, given the constraints which volume house builders adopt. It is no better at the other end of the spectrum where the modernist approach, that of the public provider and his architects, also did not give citizens what they want, providing what occupants describe as concrete barrack blocks and urban slums.

Things started well enough in public housing with estates such as the St.

The Edwardian 'semi' or pair of houses was built in huge numbers in the expanding suburbs of every English town. Street after street was lined with these well-built and attractively detailed houses with their small, neat front gardens.

Helier Estate at north Carshalton in Surrey (started in 1928) or the Old Oak Estate in Acton (started in 1911) where well-designed neo-Georgian council houses were set in generous tree-lined closes and avenues with public green spaces. This was the ethos of Hampstead Garden Suburb translated into council housing, but the malign or rather misinterpreted influence of Le Corbusier and the modernists led to the concrete estates of tower blocks set in windswept and inadequate open space, such as Fulham's wonderfully named Clem Attlee Estate of 1955 where three tall Y-plan tower blocks were crammed onto much too small a site. However, after World War II much rebuilding was in a pared down Georgian style which reached its zenith in the Festival of Britain style, so called because it thrived either side of the 1951 Festival on the South Bank in London. In this style good brickwork was combined with cement window surrounds and copings, and metal casement windows without glazing bars. It was a simple, elegant, sometimes somewhat skinny style, that was utterly vanquished in the 1960s.

Its seeds of destruction had already been sown as early as 1951 when the modern style with flats stacked in tower blocks became the norm for local authority housing, with the consequences of such social engineering all too apparent. The Alton Estate at Roehampton is an object lesson. This pioneering London County Council estate, started in 1951, set out with high ideals: the tower blocks meant you could have high densities combined with lavish open space. It was a deliberate escape, so it was hoped, from the artisan terrace housing it replaced which was seen as out of date and socially undesirable. It all went rather sadly wrong and the old working class communities were broken up to no purpose. Tower blocks of public housing were an English interpretation of Le Corbusier's Unite d'Habitation designs for villages in the sky: each block was to have its own shopping streets inside with community facilities and so on. In England (and, it has to be said, in municipal housing in France itself) costs were cut and the idealistic plans for new communities within these blocks were temporised or abandoned. They just became high blocks of flats with their occupants marooned beyond broken lifts and vandalised entrance foyers, blighted by under-maintenance and the consequences of shoddy or failed innovatory building techniques.

Architectural lessons take a long time to learn in the face of professional intransigence and continuing desires from above for social engineering. What do most people want? A house of two storeys with a garden in a suburb or the country appears to be the response and the volume house-builder seeks to provide it, however ineptly in design terms. The post-war suburban housing estate has, since the 1960s, seen a distinct tailing off in quality as the need to provide huge numbers of dwellings has met a craft crisis in which the older craftsman builders have retired to exacerbate skills shortages. Gardens and rooms have got smaller as the price of building land has risen while constraints such as Green Belts prevent the inter-war sprawl which paradoxically put fairly spacious houses within reach of clerks and the lower middle classes.

▨ INTER-WAR HOUSING ▨

The 20th century is to many such a period of extraordinary diversification and confusion that little overall pattern can be discerned. But in the early years there was the occasional flurry of individuality, such as in the curved lines of the Art Deco or the flat-roofed forms of the International Modern, both of the 1920s and 1930s. Perhaps the golden age to many is indeed this inter-war period when a booming population could be catered for by skilled designers and craftsmen. It is fashionable to sneer at Stockbroker Tudor, Metroland semi-detached houses and the like. However, they still sell quickly and remain considerably more popular than modernistic solutions.

Most readers will have an idea of the near-standard inter-war mass housing. It will be a semi-detached house with two, or more usually three, bedrooms, an upstairs bathroom, sometimes a separate lavatory, and downstairs two reception rooms and a kitchen. Sometimes there will be a scullery or larder. There will be a front garden big enough for a patch of lawn and a couple of trees while the back garden will be long, averaging about 60 feet. So far so good. The streets will be laid out with grass verges with trees such as laburnums or cherries and there will be parades of shops, a pub and often a commuter railway station. It is this last that usually made living in these suburban estates practical. Generally speaking, the working classes were living nearer the centres of towns in pre-1914 properties, terraces and small semi-detached houses. In the North they may have been back-to-backs and were certainly not as salubrious as those aspired to and occupied by the lower-middle and middle classes. To many the inside bathroom and plumbing were the height of luxury and many of the estate developments were actively promoted for their healthy environments away from the soot and fumes of the city centres, such as Muswell Hill in London or the Metroland estates of outer north-west London in which railway companies played major roles. They encouraged development, extolling the rural tranquillity but immediately filling that rural idyllic landscape of fields, hedges and woods with suburban semis, the occupants of which took their trains into the cities.

Architecturally, however, the choice with which to cloak the suburban semi was immense, and earned itself the epithet 'By-Pass Variegated'. It tended to be scorned by the architectural profession, social commentators, planners, politi-

One of the last recognisable 'styles of its time' is that of the pre-war semi-detached, with its distinctive bay windows, sometimes with curved glass in the corner sections, in the Deco style.

cians and all manner of the great and good but, and it is a big but, the occupiers and the ordinary people loved it. They bought them by the thousand, in itself a radical change and the start of the mortgage-holding society, as against the previous predominance of renting living accommodation. This in itself made for more stable and less fluid communities in the suburbs where the membership of a local tennis club might change little over twenty years. So, the lower middle and the middle classes voted with their feet and wallets, despite the clucking disapproval of those who thought they knew better what was good for people.

You could select Tudor influences: leaded light windows, timber-framed gables and steep tiled roofs with colour-washed roughcast or pebble-dashed walls; you could select Art Deco: steel windows with horizontal glazing bars, often curving round bay windows or corners, sun-burst doorways, green glazed tile roofs or, even more daring, flat roofs behind parapets. Almost all of the fully developed suburban semis had bay windows as their main frontage feature and there was much elaboration of the entrances beside them. The front door might be set behind a brick arched recessed porch with Mansion-polished quarry tiles, or an external porch or door hood. The variety was immense. You could have a Queen Anne feel, a sort of simplified Bedford Park style, and the amount of applied timber-framing and tile hanging could be more or less according to taste. Occasionally there was something more exotic with battlements to part of the house, turrets, onion domes, cupolas, circular towers: almost anything the mind of man could devise and build to a cost.

Many purchased from the drawing board before a single brick had been laid and in these circumstances the idea of choosing options and finishes led to all sorts of oddities. Inside you could find exposed beams, tiled brick fireplaces, stained glass and tiled bathrooms. The key point was the curious nonsense of individuality amid mass conformity: when you shut the front door of your small 'Jacobethan' palace behind you were an individual. Individuality was expressed by paint colours, garden walls and gates and a myriad of subtle marks and features. The architectural forms were, on the whole, strong enough to take this, unlike the modern housing estate where individuality runs absolute riot, often to the detriment of those around. This may be a response to buildings that do not achieve what the inter-war semi undoubtedly did.

Perhaps future generations will identify and select the best on offer for preservation and appreciation. Those of us seeking a home of charm and individuality, a house that reflects the needs and aspirations of those who live in it and tells us something of local skills, styles and materials, may look back to the buildings of past centuries as discussed in this book. However, for most of us it will be the houses that copy the styles we cannot afford that will have to do: that is the pre-war semi or the post-war house.

But that does not mean we should not respect the modern house and its qualities. The inter-war and Edwardian house, and indeed those up to the early 1960s, owed much in their design to established architectural practice. They were on the whole built by craftsmen who had served apprenticeships and were well trained. They had an instinctive eye for proportion and knew how to produce well-detailed buildings. These qualities are well worth conserving with just as serious an approach as with an earlier historic building. Their window proportions are important, their doors, roof tiles and wall finishes equally so. It is to be hoped that the qualities of this period are appreciated before it is too late and a sea of plastic windows and doors and miracle textured coatings, concrete roof tiles and all the other baggage of 'home improvement' sweeps it all away.

2

THE HOUSE IN
ITS REGION

Introduction

When we think of early houses – of the 15th, 16th and 17th centuries, say – the picture most likely to spring to mind is that of the timber houses: the top-heavy, jettied, check-by-jowl well-mellowed homes standing proud in the village or countryside.

Wood, however, was by no means the universal building material. The poor could seldom afford the substantial timbers needed to build a house that would last, nor the services of carpenter and wright. They made do with lowlier materials like light timber, mud and clay. In the days of difficult transport the key to understanding vernacular architecture is to realise that it depends on local materials, locally used. Thus in stone areas stone was used, in chalk areas chalkstone and flints, where good clay is found there is cob. All these local materials give areas their character. Even when brick and clay tiles arrived, because they were produced in small works using local clays the character and appearance of the brick varied from locality to locality. Indeed, all around the country, especially where wood was scarce, even the better off used what was most easily to hand: stone, perhaps, or flints, or again, clay. Only the very top echelons of society could bear the cost of transporting building materials from afar.

So there are distinctive regional traditions in building and localised styles that often continued for centuries, little altered by changing fashions. Such fashions, it is true, might influence the building of the great houses, where money and distance – for shipping materials – were no object; and details would certainly slowly seep into the smaller homes. But the appearance of many an everyday English house would for generations have depended primarily on its location, on the economic prosperity – or lack of it – of the regions, and above all on the building materials plentiful locally.

It was not until the 19th century, with the railways making brick and slate universally and cheaply available, that such regional variations began to disappear. Happily, in many of our towns and villages much evidence of earlier styles remains.

The main features of the regional styles are outlined here, and further details of building materials and techniques are to be found in other chapters, notably those on roofs and walls.

Southern England

Travelling across southern England from Cornwall to Kent, it is easy to discern the overwhelming influence of locally available materials: stone dominates in the sparsely wooded far south-west, but moving eastwards mud and clay soon take over, to be replaced in their turn by timber-framing in the well treed south and south-east. It should be stressed that this survey relates to surviving buildings, which in earlier periods tend to be at a higher social level – the prosperous farmer or squire for the most part, although odd medieval small farmhouses do survive, such as the longhouses in Devon and small timber-framed ones further east in Sussex, Surrey and Kent. Not until the 17th century do peasant houses and ordinary cottages begin to survive in significant numbers. In any case this survey is a dramatically simplified picture and you will undoubtedly find villages where all sorts of materials happily co-exist side by side.

This section starts with what was once a universal material for houses: mud. Indeed, mud walled houses are so common in Devon that 'cob', the local term for the mixture of mud, grit and straw used, has come to be applied to the variations of mud based walls found elsewhere in England too. Such houses were once common over the whole of the southern region but they have now practically disappeared in places like Kent, where people were later wealthy enough to replace them with timber and brick buildings.

Devon cob walls need to be thick to hold up the roof – several feet thick at the base, tapering gradually towards the top. The most obvious characteristics of a cob cottage are its rounded corners and deeply recessed doors and windows, which are generally few in number. The outside walls were protected against the weather by successive coats of limewash or sand-lime render and the house was given 'a good hat', originally of thatch but later of tile and nowadays even of corrugated iron, although in Devon and Cornwall often replaced with slates.

These two counties, incidentally, saw the early use of slate as it occurs naturally in the region, the quarry of Delabole in Cornwall being a notable supplier. West Country slate is still produced but the industry fell into decline when cheaper Welsh slates became more plentiful in the late 18th and early 19th centuries. In Cornwall the local variation of cob is 'clob', in which bits of broken

A typical West Country cob cottage. Cob is the local name for the mixture of mud, grit and straw used for the walls. These houses are characterised by their thick walls, rounded corners and deeply recessed doors and windows. Usually, as this example, they are thatched but in Devon and Cornwall, where slate occurs naturally, some had slate roofs long before Welsh slate was readily available throughout England.

slate are added to strengthen the muddy mixture. Devon still has hundreds of cob houses and cottages and although few of those surviving are much more than 200 years old, there are older ones such as the largest cob house in the county, Sir Walter Raleigh's birthplace at Hayes Barton, which dates from the 16th century.

Both rough stone and cob walling place restrictions on the size of houses and often extra accommodation is provided by building extensions or 'outshuts', covered by a lean-to roof sloping almost to the ground.

In the counties of Somerset, Dorset, Wiltshire and Hampshire cob houses are again much in evidence although with subtle differences from those further west. The earth here contains more chalk, and the lime in this both helps hardening and gives the walls a white appearance. It also allows them to be much thinner, often down to 18 inches, than in Devon where dung often had to be added as a binder. In Dorset, especially, local heather was substituted for straw in the cob mixture, while in the New Forest in the 19th century some walls were built of *pisé de terre*, in which earth is rammed between shutters to form walls.

Moving on to stone, the stone houses of the south-west, particularly Cornwall, are mostly built of granite. Although hard and durable, it is difficult to work, so while some of the better houses were built with well-dressed blocks, it was commonest to use rough hewn stones, often with rubble infilling. For straightness and strength however, dressed stones were used at the corners. Houses with dry stone walls are also still to be found in Cornwall. The difficulty in working the local stone accounts for the notable lack of carved detail in the ordinary houses of the area.

The upland regions of Devon and Cornwall also saw the early development of 'longhouses' to shelter both the farmer's family and his livestock under the same long roof. Such houses were subsequently altered to provide extra living space, the animals being housed elsewhere. Other characteristics to watch out for are tall, tapering chimneys (to be seen particularly on Dartmoor and in Cornwall) and a large rounded projection on house fronts, which originally contained an oven.

There is good building stone in these central southern counties too, and it is much easier to work than granite, so many houses built with well dressed stone still stand, some surviving from as early as the 15th century. They can be built taller than the West Country cob cottages: two full storeys to the eaves compared with the one-and-a-half common in cob (half of the upper room's height being contained in the roof space). Dorset had brown limestone and dark grey Purbeck stone, much favoured in churches and used in domestic architecture mainly on the Isle of Purbeck. Purbeck stone laminates well and could be split for use as roofing slates and was in great demand elsewhere in Dorset. Portland stone, used by Wren for St Paul's, comes from Dorset too, but it was little used locally, being too expensive and hard to work. Both Portland and Purbeck stone, being quarried close to the sea, could have a wider than local distribution and Portland was particularly sought after for high quality work. Wiltshire has the milky Chilmark stone and the fine Greensand while Somerset has the famous Bath stone, richly creamy and used not only in building the 18th century heart of the town but on into the late 19th century as well, and Hamstone of similar high quality.

In the Middle Ages this Central Southern section was well wooded, and as one moves eastwards there is an increasing preponderance of timber-framed houses. However, a word of caution: it seems that in most of the stone towns and villages we see now as being characteristic of the stone areas, the Great Rebuilding, whenever it took place, replaced timber houses by stone ones. So the picture is a complex one. Away from the stone areas the Great Rebuilding used timber and later on brick. As in most things nothing is as simple as it

61

seems, but this survey concentrates on what survives rather than what went before.

But whether the building was of timber or of stone, the usual roofing material was thatch. Although the high-quality Norfolk reed or water reed was sometimes used, the commonest material was a local variation of combed wheat, known as Dorset reed, or a long straw, mainly for peasant cottages and farm-buildings (for thatching materials and techniques, see p 86).

Kent, Surrey and Sussex have long enjoyed prosperity and so still contain a wealth of fine old houses in timber, stone and brick, some surviving from the 13th and 14th centuries. These counties were originally densely wooded and timber-framed houses of all kinds abound. Equally there are local clays suitable for brick making, so some of the earliest brick-built houses in the country are here too, with particularly fine red brick Tudor houses. There is stone to be found also, notably sandstone around East Grinstead, Bargate stone and the pale Kentish Ragstone, seen particularly in the Maidstone area.

The Wealden house (full details p 16) is probably the best known house type of the area, but is only one of all manner of shapes, sizes and designs of timbered buildings to be found in the south-eastern counties. Generally the earlier the house, the more heavily-timbered it will be, for by the 17th century timber supplies were becoming scarcer, not only because of the demands made by housing but also because so much charcoal was being made for use in iron smelting, begun here in Norman times. Whether heavily or light timbered however, houses in the south-east tend to be plainer in decoration and with less elaboration of the timber-framing than the more exuberant ones in, for instance, the Midlands and the North-West.

Later on weatherboarding is to be found particularly along the Kent and Sussex coasts, where it was much used in the 19th century, both to cover up the light timber studwork of new buildings or to cover the exposed timbers of medieval houses in the interests of changing fashions. An alternative technique was to tile-hang the walls, making them very durable and weatherproof but giving a feeling of bulkiness to the property. Tile hanging became a widespread practice in the 17th century as the new brickyards turned out large quantities of tiles as well as bricks. Mathematical tiles, hanging tiles that imitate brick, are found in Sussex, Wiltshire, Hampshire and Surrey, although it is unclear why this is so. Well executed mathematical tiles are quite difficult to tell from real brickwork.

Although thatch was used in these parts, a more characteristic early roofing material was stone slabs, requiring heavy timbers to support their weight. 'Horsham slabs', from the quarries near the town, found their way over much of Sussex and are still to be seen, although unfortunately all too often the appearance of such fine old roofs has been spoiled (although the weatherproofing improved) by pointing between the slates. Tiled roofs are also very common and are less steeply pitched than the stone ones.

Eastern Counties

T he essential features of the typical old house in East Anglia and eastern England are timber-framing, external plaster and big chimneys. As in the South-East, early prosperity meant many good quality houses were built – and large numbers are still to be seen. The isolation of the area from the rest of England, until comparatively recent times, has also meant distinct regional styles, and the region was also subjected, perhaps more than any-where else in the country, except perhaps not surprisingly Kent, to Continental influences, particularly from the Low Countries.

Suffolk is particularly rich in architectural history. Again once well timbered and especially wealthy in the Middle Ages with profits from the booming wool trade, it probably contains more fine timber-frame houses than any other coun-ty. Here the hall and crosswing hall house was the norm, as against the Wealden house with its continuous roof which is an occasional migrant from Kent into Essex and Suffolk. Timber-framed houses can be seen at their best in Lavenham, a town that has become a showpiece of medieval architecture. It was left largely unaltered after its rapid decline in prosperity at the end of the wool boom.

Most Lavenham houses have exposed timbers but during the 16th century it was common practice in Suffolk, and elsewhere in East Anglia, to cover both the wattle and daub panels and the supporting timbers with plaster. Mixed with hair and dung for strength, it could be scored with combs into decorative patterns, or be moulded into intricate shapes and designs, in a technique known as par-getting (see Walls, page 108). Particularly good examples of this kind of work are to be found in and around Ipswich, notably at The Ancient House, and in Saffron Walden in Essex. The centre of Ipswich, incidentally, also contains some richly carved timber houses. (For an example of a rendered timber pargetted house see p 25.)

Many plastered Suffolk houses are pink in colour, this 'Suffolk Pink' being originally a mixture of whitewash and the blood of cattle. Nowadays those want-ing to keep the traditional colours are able to buy paints and washes with less gruesome ingredients.

East Anglia also contains some of the earliest brick houses in England, a reflection of those Continental influences, especially via Flemish immigrants

East Anglia is noted for its wealth of timber-framed buildings and fine pargetting, but in the northern parts of Norfolk and Lincolnshire there is a traditional style of flint and brick construction. Like most regional variations of buildings, much depended on which materials were available locally to set the style.

who brought brick and tile making techniques over with them. They introduced new styles too, notably in the curved and shouldered 'Dutch gables' to be seen on many a 17th century brick house.

The timber tradition of Suffolk rapidly gives way to brick in the Fens, although few of the buildings there are very old since it was a sparsely populated area until it was fully drained in the 18th century. Among Peterborough's claims to fame is that it now has the biggest brickworks in the country nearby.

In north Norfolk, too, few timber houses are to be seen because of the local scarcity of wood. Here the traditional walling material was flint often simply laid roughly shaped and in irregular courses, but not infrequently neatly 'dressed' and, combined with bricks, worked into pleasing geometrical patterns. (Details of flint walling techniques on p 102.) Houses of cobbles and pebbles are also to be found, but few other stone-built houses are to be seen in the area, simply because it is not locally available. There is some chalk stone and inferior stone such as Septaria around Colchester, but broadly speaking this is not good stone country.

A relatively uncommon walling technique found in 19th century East Anglia was the use of clay lump or 'bats' – mixtures of clay and straw moulded into bricks and laid in courses, with damp clay used as mortar between them. As it is vulnerable to the weather, clay lump must be protected with a layer of plaster or roughcast, so it is often difficult to identify a clay lump house, or distinguish it from a rendered timber-framed one. It was also quite common for these houses and cottages to be given an outer skin of brick.

The Continental influences are to be seen in East Anglian roofs too, in the curved pantiles that are common in the area – both red in colour and, often in Norfolk and Suffolk, glazed black. Such pantiled roofs are pleasing (and much more interesting than the flat, dull, blue-grey slates that were to replace them), but the real glory of East Anglian roofs is thatch. Few regions can boast so many surviving thatched houses, Suffolk being particularly well endowed. The best and most beautiful thatch is that of Norfolk reed, which gives a neat and tidy finish and lasts for generations, but combed wheat reed and even long straw are the norm away from the Fens and the Norfolk Broads (see thatching materials and techniques, page 86).

Central England

The central counties of England, stretching from Nottinghamshire in the north-east to Herefordshire in the south-west, have not in the past enjoyed as great a prosperity as their neighbours in the South-East or wool boom East Anglia. The exception is of course the limestone belt from the Cotswolds into Lincolnshire where wool prosperity is reflected in huge numbers of 16th and 17th century stone houses and fine stone-built towns.

Many areas have relatively few houses of sufficient quality to have withstood the passage of time. Nonetheless there are still some fine old houses and – in some areas, notably the Cotswolds and in Shropshire – there are delightful local styles found nowhere else. Only in the central Midlands, densely populated as a result of the Industrial Revolution, is the paucity of ancient houses really noticeable.

In the rural parts of central Britain, one very pleasing aspect is the preservation of older buildings in their original settings, stranded by the ebb of local prosperity. In rich times a village of fine houses could spring up, but as times again became hard, there would be little further development or even alteration. Many of the stone villages in the Cotswolds, for example, have been preserved by this process. It was not, however, necessarily a rapid affair. Although the uniformity of design in many a Cotswold village seems to imply that all the houses were built in the same period, the style varied very little for two or three centuries. Both prosperity and decline could have occurred over long periods. So a house with gabled dormers rising out of its front walls, stone mullioned windows and coped parapetted side walls – a typical Cotswold style – may have an Elizabethan look to it, but could well have been built in the 18th century.

The small towns and villages, built in the richly coloured local oolitic limestone blend perfectly and timelessly with their surroundings and the feeling of naturalness is frequently enhanced by the lichen covering the stone-tiled roofs. Prime examples (and there are many others) are Cirencester, Stow-on-the-Wold, Chipping Campden and Burford. At the other end of the limestone belt, which provided readily available, easily workable building stone, lie Warwickshire with its brown (iron-rich) Hornton stone, then Northamptonshire and Lincolnshire, with their creamier limestones, including the superb Clipsham, Ancaster and Barnack stones. Towns built in it include, outstandingly, Stamford in Lincolnshire and Oundle in Northamptonshire.

The style of the stone Cotswold dormered cottage varied very little over two or three centuries. Sometimes they were thatched, but more often, as in this example, the houses were roofed with local stone tiles, giving a feeling of naturalness and harmony with its surroundings.

In the central region, due to excellent local clays, brick making began early: from 1600 onwards bricks were used to build great mansions in the south Midlands. But timber was not forgotten and triumphs in timber-frame building are still to be found, notably in Shropshire, where a feature is heavy ornamentation and elaborate design. Architecturally the two most important towns in the area are Ludlow and Shrewsbury, each containing fine examples of flamboyant timber-frame building. The famous Feathers Hotel in Ludlow shows the style in its extreme, well over half the wall being covered in deeply-carved timber. Not quite so ornate, but still magnificently imposing, is Ireland's Mansions in Shrewsbury, a four-storeyed 16th century house with heavily-beamed bays and dormers.

In neighbouring Herefordshire, a characteristic is very heavy framing timbers, and the country also contains fine examples of late timber buildings, as do Worcestershire and Warwickshire, for here the timber tradition stood out longer against the change to brick. Dense woodland, a soil ideally suited to oak trees and until the mid 18th century less demand for charcoal for ironmaking than in the South-East seem to have kept the timber tradition alive longer. Some say the distance from the sea helped, for the great demands for ship building timber in the later 17th and 18th centuries certainly had an impact on the oak woods of the coastal counties such as Sussex and Hampshire.

Northern Region

T he northernmost counties of England were originally thinly populated and far fewer houses were built here before the 18th century than elsewhere in the country. Not until the Industrial Revolution was there any major expansion in population and building. Rather like Scotland there were few peasant houses of any substance until the 18th century and earlier cottages do not survive because of their light materials. In the Highland Zone, of course, trees suitable for building timber are sparse while in other areas timber houses have long been replaced by brick or stone ones.

Timber-framing of medieval and 17th century dates does survive in isolated examples but by and large most towns only saw sufficient wealth for rebuilding from the 18th century onwards and this swept away the older timber-framed houses. For example Beverley in Yorkshire was a noted timber-built town in the 17th century, but now only traces remain. In the Pennines and the uplands stone houses survive in numbers, particularly at manorial and yeoman level, such as the Old Hall of 1650 and Old Hall Farm of 1630 in Youlgreave, Derbyshire.

Although timber-framed buildings are scarce there are large numbers of cruck houses extant, many of them in Wales, the Pennines and the North York Moors. These are often survivals of peasant houses so are a direct link with the pre-brick and pre-stone building periods. There are a couple of exceptions to this scarcity of recognisable timber-framing: Chester, Cheshire and the City of York. York, as England's second city, had long commercial, political and ecclesiastical importance, and was full of timber-framed buildings. Many of these now hide behind Georgian brick re-facings, but others are relatively unaltered, as in The Shambles, a medieval street of overhanging jettied houses.

Cheshire, which perhaps really belongs to the Central Region but links the highland zones of Wales and England, is famous for its elaborate black and white timber houses, enhanced with curved wooden braces and diagonals across the whitewashed panels. Such magnificent 'magpie work' however, was usually confined to larger houses, of which Little Moreton Hall (1559) is the most famous example. Cheshire still also contains some fine examples of cruck houses (see page 13). It was a favourite style in timbered areas of the region even for bigger houses.

In parts of the north, after the longhouse in which animals and the owner shared the same building, the laithe house emerged where a barn or cowhouse was built under the same roof or attached to the house. They became the traditional home of the hill farmer and his family.

In Chester itself, the most striking timber buildings are The Rows, with continuous galleried walkways at first floor level. Originally houses of wealthy merchants, most of the surviving ones date from the 15th and 16th centuries, although most of the framing you see now is Victorian replacement and renovation.

As one travels further north, however, timber houses become much scarcer, and stone takes over. Regional variations in design are determined more by the qualities of the stone and how easily it can be worked than by fashion. Because of the area's remoteness, change in style was a slow business anyway and often there was little variation for generations. Any changes that did occur, came much later than in the south so caution is needed when trying to date the stone houses of the north. They may well appear, stylistically, to be a century or so older than they actually are.

In the north-west of the area, sandstone dominates. Being relatively easy to work it allows building in well fashioned blocks (called ashlar) or regular courses, and was routinely sawn to produce fine joints. Towards the Pennines, however, millstone grit, a much harder and more brittle stone, takes over – and here the houses tend to have rubble walls (mortared or sometimes even dry stone) with well dressed blocks used only at the corners and around the doors and windows. On the north-east coastal plain, softer stone – limestone – reappears and with it houses in better fashioned blocks or stone courses.

The stone gives colour to the older buildings of the region: pinkish reds in the sandstone area, the greys of the millstone grit which tend to blacken in the air, and the pale-grey limestones of Yorkshire and Durham. In the Lake District local slate was used, both for roofs and in dry-stone walling, and locally found volcanic stone – tuff – gives a pleasant greenish look to houses in the area.

The oldest houses of the region are the longhouses, the traditional dwellings of the hill farmer and his family (and, initially, his animals). Built low and squat as protection against the weather, the longhouse has a shallow-pitched roof, covered with slates or more commonly, originally at least, with stone slabs. The chimney is squat too, and often with the windproofing cover of a pair of stone slabs or slates in the shape of an inverted 'V'. In many of the older houses the size of the stone blocks was massive in relation to the wall, giving a rather curious appearance but nonetheless great longevity and a capacity to withstand the roughest weather.

In the 16th and 17th century farmhouses on the coastal plains, stone mullioned windows were a feature and are still to be seen, although unfortunately their sandstones are often eroded by polluted air.

In the counties abutting the Scottish borders – Cumberland and Northumberland – the longhouse gave way to the tower house, a fortified bastion against border raiders and cattle reavers. Known as bastle or pele houses, these square or rectangular towers rose to two or three storeys. In the earlier ones, built from the 13th century onwards, living accommodation was on the first floor, with cattle beneath; while in later ones, built up to the 17th century, all the house was used for human accommodation. Almost all the tower houses that survive have been altered or incorporated into larger houses. One interesting group are known as vicar's peles, because they were used as clergymen's houses. They were built near churches, which were also targets for cross border raids and examples are to be found at Corbridge and at Alnham, Elsdon, Embleton, Ford and Whitton.

By the 17th century brick was to be seen increasingly everywhere and in both the east and west coastal plains there were good clays for brickmaking. Through the 17th and 18th centuries the local bricks were hand-made and fired in clamps, until machine-made bricks became available at the turn of the 19th century. To the east of the Pennines brick took over during the 18th century, except on the limestone where stone continued in use. Towns like Malton came to present a brick face to the world. In the west the Industrial Revolution produced a desperate need for huge numbers of cheap houses and mass produced bricks met this demand in the boom towns of central Lancashire. In the early 19th century machine-made bricks were manufactured in huge numbers, and the local clays produced the characteristic vivid red bricks of the area, of which 'Accrington Bloods' are an example. The population boom in Yorkshire towns like Huddersfield was largely met by local stone quarries, although brick increasingly appeared with stone reserved for the quoins, window heads and arches.

In the Lake District and its surrounding area houses are generally built in slatey, rubbly hard irregular stone, often whitewashed or rendered, while on the coastal plain around the Solway Firth cob reappears. In fact cob pops up everywhere on our journey north from Southern England: in Buckinghamshire, Northamptonshire, Leicestershire and Lincolnshire particularly, so it is a fitting finish to this brief survey of the house in its regions.

3

THE HOUSE
IN DETAIL

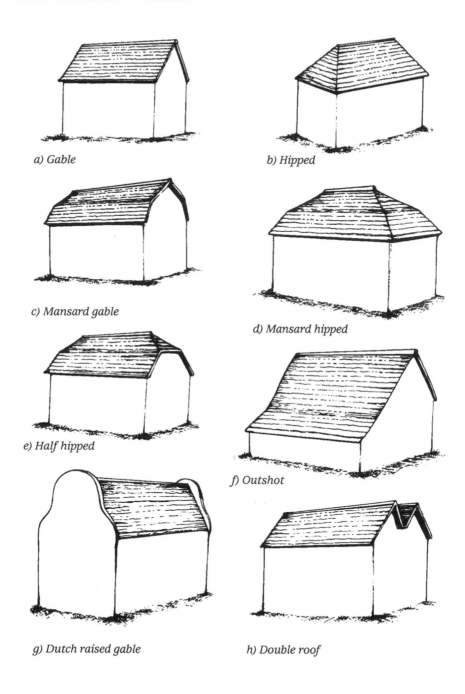

a) Gable

b) Hipped

c) Mansard gable

d) Mansard hipped

e) Half hipped

f) Outshot

g) Dutch raised gable

h) Double roof

The Roof

T he roof is the most important structure in any house and also the most difficult to raise both safely and soundly. As well as combating the force of gravity, which wants to pull the construction tumbling downwards, the builder has to contend with outward pressures, which tend to make the roof splay. For the cathedral and church master builder supporting his high and vast roofs with pillars and soaring masonry, thickening the walls into buttresses was the solution to containing these outward thrusts. Later when he had to deal with the massive thrusts from heavy stone vaults below the timbers of the roof the elegant flying buttress solved the problem of keeping the walls from bursting outwards.

For the house builder the ultimate and simplest answer was to hold the roof together internally by tying the rafters together at their feet with timber beams to form a triangle. This effectively neutralised much of the thrust and, provided the 'tie beam' is intact, there should be relatively little problem. However, if the tie beam is raised above the base of the triangle, that is slid up the rafters, the equilibrium is disturbed and the natural tendency of the rafters to spread outwards reasserts itself. A variety of designs to resolve these problems evolved over the centuries but the basic techniques developed by the early carpenters can still be recognised in the construction of our roofs today.

▓ EARLY ROOFS ▓

The house of the English peasant, it seems, varied very little from early Saxon times right to the end of the Middle Ages. We lack precise details because the earliest timber houses still standing date from the 13th century, but from earlier remains, and from historical accounts, we can build up a picture of the very earliest dwellings.

There are two basic components to a roof: the raftering, or supporting structure, and the covering, generally known in early times as 'thatch', whatever the material used.

A rafter is simply a wooden pole and for most of Prehistoric Britain, thick with forest, poles of all shapes and sizes and suppleness were readily available.

As for the thatch, archaeologically, evidence of roof covering rarely survives, but turf, heather, bracken, reeds or straw could have been used depending on availability. Many Iron Age houses, whether stone or timber, oval or circular, had internal or external porches. The occurrence of the latter would have affected roofing.

The problem with a circular structure is that, unless the roof pitch is steep and the side walls of reasonable height, the usable vertical space is small compared with the horizontal area enclosed. Excavated round houses and modern reconstructions have shown that they could have diameters of about thirty feet with the rafters lashed to a tall central post.

Although there had been Roman architectural influence before their conquest of Britain in the first century AD, the Roman administration brought with it revolutionary techniques in town design and house construction. The Roman carpenter with his well-fashioned tools could construct strong rectangular frameworks for a variety of buildings in legionary fortresses and army camps, the newly founded or rebuilt towns and in the villas scattered around the countryside. These buildings frequently boasted clay tile or stone slate roofs.

At the end of the Roman period, as the administrative and economic organisation broke down, the towns and villas fell into decay. However, they were far from abandoned and many towns survived the earlier Anglo-Saxon conquests at varying levels of occupation. It is difficult to believe that London was ever abandoned and many towns have Anglo-Saxon architectural remains, for instance Colchester and Cambridge. The list of Roman towns that are still towns or cities today belies earlier views of complete abandonment and in the countryside many of the Roman farmsteads survived and their estate boundaries form the basis of medieval villages, manors and parishes.

The point is that the Anglo-Saxon conquerors found fine buildings here, albeit many were ruinous, and they had great admiration for them. There is evidence in contemporary documents of visiting dignitaries being given guided tours of old Roman towns, such as Carlisle, by Anglo-Saxon officials. Thus the Anglo-Saxon had the examples of standing buildings from a more architecturally advanced society all around him as well as the traditions he brought from abroad.

What also seems certain is that although the round house survived into Roman Britain, the Anglo-Saxons never used it. In Anglo-Saxon England two styles emerged – the sunken hut, and the hall. The sunken hut, known in Germany as a *grubenhaus*, has its floor sunk in the ground to a depth of up to three feet. Sometimes, as at Mucking in Essex, there is evidence that these sunken floors were the actual occupation level – giving maximum usable space for the minimum building materials. The turves seem to have provided walling materials for the longer side walls, supporting rafters leaning or lashed to a ridge beam held up by posts at each end and in the middle, and roofed with straw, bracken or turves. Sometimes, as at West Stow in Suffolk where Anglo-Saxon houses and huts have been re-constructed, the sunken area seems to have been an underfloor pit with the occupation floor at ground level above it. However, there is considerable doubt that these sunken huts were anything more than workshops and storehouses: in many excavations loom weights have been found. Indeed many of these sunken huts were frequently ancillary to a larger ground level building, and it was this latter which formed the starting point for the medieval building tradition.

The grandest manifestation of this was the great hall. (For a sectional drawing of a later aisled hall house showing the roof construction see p 8.) The roof rafters of squared timbers were on an impressive scale, supported not only by the stout posts and planking of the walls but also by an elaborate ancillary system of oak posts and beams which gave additional strength. The chief distinction between these early buildings and the later medieval ones was that the posts were mostly what is known as 'earth-fast', that is they went directly into the ground, rather than resting on ground plates or continuous timbers. Much of the evidence for these Anglo-Saxon halls comes from the excavated holes for such posts, which have allowed archaeologists to reconstruct the ground plan. The roof may have been 'hipped' – that is, there were no high gable end walls but rather the thatch was carried round the ends on high rafters. Early halls appear to be almost all roof.

The basically triangular cross sectional structure was undoubtedly repeated in longhouses much smaller than the hall where the building provided shelter for the animals as well as people. Examples are known where foundation trenches for the side walls are deeper than those for the end walls – presumably because the side walls took the main weight of the roof.

The Saxon roof covering continued to be turf, bracken, reed, straw or heather, or shingles – wooden tiles made from the off-cuts when the logs were squared.

▩ THE CRUCK FRAME ▩

The essentially triangular cross section had always created problems of head room in the smaller houses in relation to ground area covered. One solution that emerged was the cruck frame. By selecting for the major roof support timbers that were slightly curved or angled, the builder could convert the triangle into an arch. The cruck thus combined the wall post with the rafter without the problem of a joint between the two – always a potential weakness. The best crucks (the word is a variation of crook) were made by selecting a tree with natural curvature or with a substantial bough curving away from the trunk and cutting it in two down the middle so that the two halves could be squared and pegged together at their apex to form a perfectly symmetrical support.

The basic module consisted of two pairs of oak crucks, set some 16 feet apart, usually supporting a horizontal ridge piece. The crucks were strengthened with cross beams or tie beams below the apex. Later medieval cruck trusses (that is pairs of crucks) were also joined by purlins: timbers set half way up the roof slope which support the rafters at their mid-point. Common rafters were then run from ridge piece to wall plate or passed over the purlin to be pegged at their apex. The walls were braced with vertical posts called studs and filled in with material like wattle and daub (of which more details in the chapter on walls). Bigger houses could be built by simply adding extra similar bays.

Crucks were usually fashioned from oak, sometimes from chestnut. Together with the other, equally bulky, timbers for tie beam, wall plate, ridge piece and the like, they were sawn and shaped in the carpenter's yard, and their joints cut out and marked up with code numbers ready for transport to the building site. Erecting the house was still very much a co-operative venture, with not only the owner's family joining in but other members of the community too, especially in the strenuous task of manhandling and levering the cumbersome crucks into position.

At first, it seems, crucks were erected without foundations, although the ends of the timbers were charred to try to help to preserve them. Later, they rested on individual stone blocks, then ground sills were used and even dwarf walls of stone or brick, to give more height to the living space and reduce damp penetrating the cruck bases.

At the apex of the cruck there were various configurations. The two curved beams might meet and be jointed and pegged together, or they might even criss-cross each other, but a common design was to span a small gap at the top with a short saddle beam, on which the longitudinal ridge piece of the roof would rest. For greater stability a collar beam was usually inserted a few feet from the apex.

There were many different arrangements, too, in the beams and timbers that helped to support the roof structures and delineate the walls. One important technique was to fix a tie beam across the crucks, at the point where they began to curve, with its ends projecting. On these rested the wall plates which in turn supported the feet of the rafters. For those carpenters who did not wish for the tie beam to divide up the internal space, they substituted short timber spurs halved or jointed from the cruck to support the wall plate, thus in effect leaving out the main section of the tie beam. These methods meant that the walls thus bore none of the pressures of the roof and could be built in light framing with wattle and daub panels or mud, although in some areas where it was readily available, stone was used too. Whatever the precise internal arrangements of the timbers, the basic arched shape of the construction gave much more headroom and at least those of more modest means – peasant farmers, say – could live in something better than a cramped hut.

In the 16th and 17th centuries there were to be further changes in cruck design and construction. Several techniques evolved so that less wood, and shorter timbers, could be used. In one arrangement the cruck started near the ground but ended well below the ridge, usually just above the collar beam, a tie beam set at the level of the purlins. By avoiding the crucks having to meet at the apex of the roof, crucks could be set further apart and this was a technique favoured in Oxfordshire, Berkshire and Buckinghamshire in particular. In another type, the arch was not formed from single timbers, but from two suitably shaped shorter lengths pegged together, a type popular in the south-west of England. (For an example of a cruck frame house see p 13.)

▓ THE BOX FRAME OR TIMBER FRAME ▓

The alternative building system is the 'box frame', but as this is now more commonly called the 'timber frame' we will normally use this term throughout the book. It is this form that predominates in the surviving earliest houses of the south and east. Again its precise origins are uncertain, but it was probably around before the Conquest: woven into the Bayeux Tapestry, for instance, appear to be pictures of box frame houses being passed by the conquering army.

The basic box frame is, as its name implies, a construction of beams and posts jointed together to form a hollow box. The four corner posts, resting on ground sills, are joined at their tops laterally by tie beams and longitudinally by wall plates. Again, bigger houses or barns could be built by repeating the module as many times as necessary.

The box has two distinct advantages over the cruck: it can support a higher roof and it can be extended sideways as well as lengthways. In mounting a roof on top of the frame the builder had, of course, to find ways to counteract the ever present tendency of his pairs of rafters to splay outwards. The tie beam, the lateral link between posts across the building did, as we have seen earlier, 'triangulate' the main rafters and thus counteract the roof thrusts. The ridge beam or the purlins were supported by posts rising from the tie beam and these were assisted by a system of wind braces. As their name implies, their function was to strengthen the box and help it resist strong winds. These braces, usually curved like half an arch, are used to brace the tie beams and wall plates where

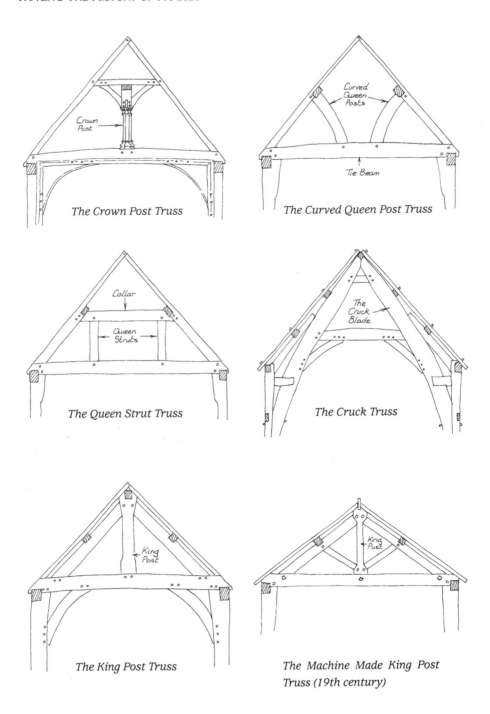

The Crown Post Truss

The Curved Queen Post Truss

The Queen Strut Truss

The Cruck Truss

The King Post Truss

The Machine Made King Post Truss (19th century)

they meet the vertical posts, and to brace the purlins and the ridge pieces. Curved or arched wind braces are characteristic of timber-framing in houses until the end of the 17th century and in barns and farm buildings for a further two centuries. (For a sectional drawing of a box frame house showing the roof construction see p 15.)

▨ ROOF TRUSSES ▨

A better solution to the problems of splaying roofs emerged with the evolution of the crown post roof. In this the ridge beam was lowered from the apex of the roof onto short posts, known as 'crown posts', rising from the centre of the tie beams. The ridge beam in its new lower location and running centrally along the length of the roof is called the 'collar purlin', for each pair of rafters had a collar beam joining them and resting on the collar purlin beam.

In this way the centre of gravity of the roof structure was lowered and the rafters, jointed at their apexes, were now also prevented from sagging under the weight of the roof covering by the collar beams a third or half way down their length. The crown post could be further strengthened by braces running to the tie beam, or to the collar beam and collar purlin, and often the posts were decoratively carved.

By the 15th century roofs reached their most structurally perfect form when the collar purlin was replaced by the side purlin style. Here the purlins were moved across to support directly the rafters at the side of the roof and were turned through 45 degrees, thus giving the rafters maximum support. The side purlin was supported by the collar beam which itself was supported by queen

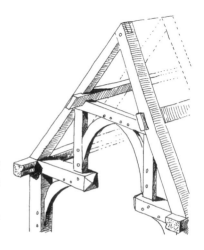

Hammer-beams were used to support the principal roof rafters without the need for tie beams. The short beams, plus the superstructure of beams, struts and braces, took the weight of the whole roof and distributed its pressure evenly.

posts or struts symmetrically placed at the outer thirds of the tie beam, in effect displacing the crown post. The side purlin roof with collar beams put the support for the rafters where it was needed most and by the mid 16th century it had supplanted the crown post roof in all but the north and west where the king post, that is a post from the centre of the tie beam up to the apex of the roof, remained popular.

The medieval carpenter also developed ways of supporting his principal rafters without the need for obstructive tie beams in the central roof space. This he did by using curved timbers in arch or scissor configurations or in perhaps the most splendid of his innovations: the hammer-beam roof. In effect the tie beam between the queen posts was cut out and arch braces supported the stubs of the tie beam while the queen post was braced to the collar beam above. The braces carried the thrusts down the wall post and its chief benefit was that a wider building could be roofed without aisle posts. It was only used, however, in the bigger houses and in grand halls, like the Pilgrim's Hall in Winchester, mid 14th century and one of the earliest hammer-beam roofs known. The magnificent Westminster Hall, built for Richard II in the 1390s, has a span of 68 feet, combining hammer beams with a giant timber arch: a most ingenious design. The hammer-beam roof's finest flowering was in the East Anglian wool churches where double and triple hammer-beam roofs soar majestically above their naves and chancels.

Many styles and systems of roof support developed, due in part to the suitability of available timber but mainly to local tradition and craft training systems, rather than to a truly scientific appreciation of all the thrusts and forces involved. Commonsense and experience were the rule of the day. By the mid 16th century the king post and queen post roof became the norm, again with a regional distribution, the former in the north and west, the latter in the south and east.

The roof supports, that is all the timbers including and surrounded by the tie beam and the principal rafters, whatever their design, are known collectively as trusses. They formed the basis of almost all roofs right through to Victorian times; house styles varied considerably through the centuries but the supporting structures beneath changed little.

There was, however, in the 18th century, one development in the way the covering was fixed. This type of roof had no common rafters: instead thin wooden boards were fixed directly to the purlins, and then slates (usually) were nailed to the boards. Never widely adopted, modern roofs continued and continue to follow the older fixing methods, using battens nailed across rafters. The only change nowadays being the use of sawn softwood laths instead of the split oak ones used into the 19th century.

The development of the steam saw in the early 19th century brought about much standardisation of roofs, for pre-cut truss beams and posts could now be turned out in large numbers. Some builders, such as Thomas Cubitt who built Mayfair, Belgravia and Pimlico, even had their own woodyards to produce the pre-fabricated pieces.

Although their essential structure altered little through the years, roofs can give us valuable clues about the date of the house beneath them: not in the covering, for that may have been changed many times, but in the principal timbers under it, for they are more likely to be original. An old house with a steeply-pitched roof, for instance, was undoubtedly originally thatched with reed or straw, even if it is tiled or slated now. The amount of timber used can give a clue too. From the late 15th century onwards, as wood became increasingly scarce, less and less was used in truss construction, so they became lighter and less ponderous. A caveat here, for the very earliest roofs found in houses use smaller scantling timbers than became the norm in the 14th to 17th centuries, so in exceptional cases slender beams may be a sign of extreme age. While oak was used almost exclusively in the 13th, 14th and 15th centuries, other woods like elm and chestnut began to replace it from the 16th century onwards and elm is commonly found in barns during the 18th century.

THE ROOF COVERING

Externally roofs come in a variety of shapes, and the roof of an old house is likely to have been altered and added to over the years. There are two basic styles: the gabled roof and the hipped roof. With the gable, the end walls extend vertically to the ridge, while in the hipped roof the vertical wall stops at the tie beam and the end of the roof itself inclines inwards. The advantage of the hip is that there is less end wall exposed to the elements; its disadvantage is that the roof structure becomes more complex and the space in the loft is lessened.

One solution to that problem is the mansard roof, first designed by the Frenchman Francois Mansard in the 17th century. Here the roof has two different pitches, the lower steeper and broader than the upper one. The mansard principle may be applied to both hipped and gabled roofs.

A great many roofs, however, are hybrids, like the half-hipped roof which allows a window in the half-gable, or the gable-hipped (or gambrel) roof. The word gambrel refers to the shape of a horse's hind leg and the small upper gable ends of these roofs, known as gablets, were originally left open or louvred to allow smoke to escape from the hall beneath.

Because of the problems of supporting a wide-span roof, early medieval houses tended to be narrow, just one room deep. The easiest way for their owners

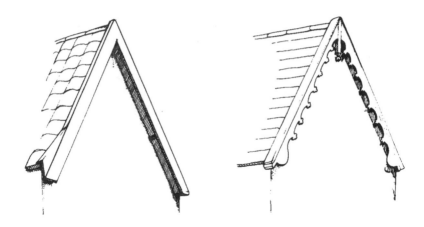

To protect the gable ends of houses which would be exposed to damage from wind and rain, barge boards were added. Early examples would be quite plain, but by the 19th century they would often be decoratively carved.

to extend them in depth was to add what amounted to a lean-to at the back, continuing the line of the original roof. Such 'outshot' roofs (sometimes called 'catslides' in the north) would often end only a couple of feet above the ground. Another alternative was to build what were effectively two narrow houses, one behind the other with the roofs taking the shape of an 'M'. In most historic roof construction the lower couple of feet were tilted or 'sprocketted' to cast rainwater further from the wall faces below. When guttering became universal sprocketting was often retained although now largely a stylistic hangover.

In gable-ended roofs, the ends of the horizontal beams of the supporting structure were often exposed to wind and rain. They were protected by timber bargeboards (or vergeboards), sometimes simple and unadorned but not infrequently carved with vigorous sweeping and interlacing designs. Another feature particular to East Anglian roofs is a thin cap fixed on top of the bargeboards, running back to overlap the first tier of tiles.

▣ Thatch

Turves were the most important of the earliest roof coverings, although moss, bracken and heather were often used. Such roofs, however, would not last many years and they were gradually superseded by a far superior product: reed and straw thatch. Before the 17th century, most ordinary houses in the country were thatched and although many old houses were re-roofed with tiles or slates, particularly in the 18th and 19th centuries, there are still plenty left in country districts.

Before the 17th century most ordinary people's homes were thatched. Norfolk reed (as the example on the right) was considered to be both beautiful and long lasting, giving a neat and tidy finish which would last for generations. Long straw thatching (as the example on the left) used straw from corn threshed by hand. The introduction of threshing machines in the mid-19th century rendered the straw useless for thatching but recently farmers have adapted their methods to leave long straw once again available for the thatcher's art.

Reed obviously commended itself from the earliest times in those areas where it was readily accessible; and as agriculture got into full swing, increasing quantities of straw were available too. Thatch's advantages are its lightness, so it does not require massive roof supports, and its good heat insulation properties, conserving the indoor heat in winter and coolness in summer. Its drawback is the fire hazard.

The three most important thatching materials are Norfolk reed, combed wheat reed and long straw.

Norfolk reed or water reed, tough and durable, is the finest thatching material of all. The reeds flourished not only in the Broadland marshes but in the Suffolk and Essex estuaries (and Dorset ones too) and in other places with low-lying saltings. The light golden reed, culled anything from 3 to 8 feet long, is less yielding than wheat reed and gives a much crisper harder line. The main snag with the material is that the roof has to be stripped back to the timbers each time while wheat reed is merely capped and can be shaped into soft and undulating contours, the perfect complement to ancient walls and timbers.

Long straw is simply threshed corn, usually wheat, although barley and rye were used. Combed wheat reed is the threshed straw further 'processed' by removing the grain head and the outer leaves to reveal smooth reed-like straws. These are more woody than the long straw and thus more durable. It was particularly popular in the south and south-east. Threshing machines ruined straw for thatching purposes and as R. W. Brunskill points out in *Vernacular Architecture*, 'there was presumably some relation between the spread of threshing machines in the north and west where other roofing materials were available, and their slow adoption in the east and south'. Nowadays special threshing machines are needed for the production of combed wheat reed and long straw.

Long straw thatching uses cruder methods than those for the finer reeds, and it could often be carried out by agricultural workers themselves, who perfected their techniques by thatching haystacks against the winter weather. Hence the scornful description by master thatchers of such men as 'rick thatchers', even when they worked on houses and cottages: there is nothing quite like the contempt of one craftsman for another.

The wetted straw was gathered into rough oval bundles, some 16 to 18 inches wide and 4 to 6 inches thick, called yealms. These were laid on battens, starting at the eaves, and held in place by long strips of hazel, the sways, which were secured through to the rafters with iron thatching hooks. The yealms were built up in overlapping courses to the ridge, giving an overall thickness of some 12 to 15 inches.

The parting of the ways at the ridge needed the extra protection of a cap made of several layers of straw bundles, again secured with hazel strips both longways and criss-crossed (liggers and crossrods). Extra liggers and crossrods were used, too, at eaves and gables. The finishing touch was to comb out or 'dress down' the unruly straw with a large wooden comb, called a side rake, and trim off with knife and shears the ragged eaves and barges.

The great advantage of reeds was that they had much greater longitudinal strength so each yealm could be 'dressed', that is, knocked into shape with the butt ends flush, as it was put up. This was done with a tool known as a leggett, a flat wooden hammer with bumps on it. Reed yealms could also be secured with sways and thatching hooks, but often skilled thatchers preferred tying them to the rafters, using a large needle to thread straw rope or tarred cords through into the roof space and back.

Combed wheat reed can be laid in the same way as long straw or water reed and is thus suitable for most areas and traditions, but away from the water reed areas only combed wheat or long straw should be used, both laid as long straw. Water reed roofs are more compact than straw or wheat reed covered ones, with a much neater close-cropped appearance. Liggers and crossrods were unnecessary at their eaves and verges. Norfolk reed, however, is not very pliable and so the ridge was capped with sedge, shaped, curved and decorated.

Thatched roofs require a steep pitch to carry rainwater safely away rather than absorbing it. Pitches vary from about 45 degrees in south-west England to 55 degrees elsewhere, or even steeper for long straw.

Reed roofs could last for a considerable time: Norfolk reed for as much as eighty to a hundred years and combed wheat reed up to sixty years. Long straw lasted less well – about twenty five years – but had the advantage that it was much easier to replace.

There is a surprising amount of medieval thatch to be found, for combed wheat and long straw roofs are usually rethatched by raking off decayed straw and capping over it, so the innermost layer is untouched. There are many surviving examples of smoke blackening and soot from medieval open hearths to be seen on the underside of straw over 500 years old.

Newer roofing materials like tile and slate at one time threatened the craft of thatching with extinction but it has now made a healthy revival.

▨ Shingles

Another ancient roof covering was shingles, wooden tiles fashioned from oak and much favoured by the Saxons. They were used quite widely up to the 15th century, when more durable clay tiles began to be available lower down the social scale, although shingled roofs as late as the 18th century can be found. Oak shingles were revived early in the 20th century but are now commonest in imported cedar and usually reserved for outbuildings.

The average shingle was some 2 feet long and about 7 inches wide – and they were hung to overlap by about 8 inches. Their lower ends would be pointed and rounded (to pull water away from the joins) and also slightly thicker than the top. The shingle roof had a lifespan of some fifty to a hundred years, during which time the oak would weather to a beautiful silvery-grey. Like reed or straw thatch, however, their great disadvantage was that they were inflammable.

▨ Stone

Stone, a strong, weatherproof and fireproof covering material, was used for roofs in those areas where workable stone for slabs was easily accessible.

Sedimentary rocks like limestone and sandstone, which can be split along their layers, are needed and these are found mainly in the Pennines, and in the Midlands, the Cotswolds, Wiltshire, Dorset, Wales and the Weald.

Stone roofing material falls into two categories: thick, heavy stone flags, basically of sandstone and used chiefly in the Pennines, and thinner and lighter stone tiles, usually limestone, found particularly in the Cotswolds and South Wales or the Wealden sandstones.

Flags can be up to 4 feet wide and 3 inches thick, and need a sturdy roof structure to support them. It is usually pitched at 30 degrees or less, but even so the roof remains weather-proof because of the large overlap of each row. The lighter tiles were laid on a much steeper pitch – 50 degrees or even more and could be used on much more intricate roof shapes than the ponderous flags.

Both were fixed in basically the same way, being pegged into stout laths secured to the rafters. A hole was drilled near the top of the flag or tile and a peg of oak (or in the Lake District, sheep's bone) hammered home through it. The tops of the slabs were generally rounded or V-shaped, which helped to reduce the weight, but failure of the pegs was a common problem, as was erosion of the undersides of the slabs. Both flags and tiles were traditionally laid in graduated sizes, the largest at the eaves and the smallest at the ridge, although tile sizes vary less than flags.

To complete the waterproofing the stones were often bedded on moss and 'torched' on their undersides, that is, painted with a mixture of clay and hair. Later torching was done with lime mortar.

In parts of the north it was common practice to use a combination of stone flags and pantiles for the roof, laying three or four courses of heavy slabs over the wall near the eaves for solidity and protection against 'windlift' but covering the rest of the roof with lighter pantiles. In Dorset and the Cotswolds, similarly, stone tiles were often laid for the courses immediately over the wall and the rest of the roof was clad in plain clay tiles.

▦ Tiles

Although the Romans were great tile makers, the tradition faltered, and reed or straw thatch continued to dominate roof coverings for most of England's houses until well into the 17th century. It was, of course, a great fire hazard in the towns. As early as 1212, for example, Londoners had been forbidden to roof their houses with 'Straw, Reeds, Rushes or Strubble'. Fired clay tiles, at first imports from the Low Countries, were available in the early 13th century, but they remained expensive to produce and were generally used higher up the social scale. Not until new, more economical techniques were introduced in the 17th century could they really compete with thatch. These developments

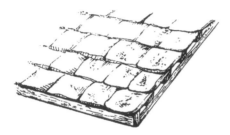

a) Stone tiles were an early roofing material, most commonly in Kent, Sussex and the Cotswolds. They were nailed or pegged on battens and required heavy roof timbers to support their weight.

b) Fired clay tiles were first imported from the Low Countries as early as the 13th century, but only became a common roofing material when mass-produced tiles developed alongside brickmaking in the 17th century.

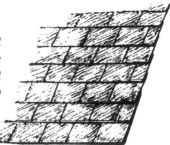

c) Clay pantiles began to appear in the 17th century, initially imported from Holland. They are most commonly found in eastern and north-eastern counties and Somerset.

d) With the development of canal and railway transport slate roofs became popular. Regular in shape, light and tough, a slate roof could last up to 100 years.

marched hand in hand with the advances in brickmaking, increasing numbers of tiles being turned out also by the expanding brickyards.

There are two basic types of tile: the plain, or flat tile and the curved pantile.

The plain tile's size – 10½ inches long by 6½ inches wide and half an inch thick – was standardised in 1479, but its early use, like that of bricks, was largely confined to the south, south-east and the Midlands, where slate or stone alternatives were not readily available. The plain tile is not actually flat but slightly curved, to help speed the water across its surface, and the old hand-made tiles with all their individual variations give ancient roofs a delightful undulating surface which roofs of mass produced tiles entirely lack.

The tiles were hung on light battens of split oak laths or of sawn softwood, using oak pegs or nails through holes in the upper part of the tile, or, more recently, resting on 'nibs', small clay bumps moulded onto their upper edges. Each plain tile overlapped two others beneath it, so that only about 4 inches of the tile's 10½ inches was exposed to the elements. Specially moulded tiles to fit snugly into the 'valleys' of a roof and sweep round its hips, allowed quite complex roof structures to be covered. Half-round tiles capped the ridge and special bonnet tiles were also made for covering the hip corners.

Some tile makers and house builders enjoyed bringing bright patterns to their roofs with multi-coloured tiles, or picking out the date of building; and there were also more intricately shaped tiles (fish-scales, for instance) which created pleasing patterns.

Pantiles are really a development of the interlocking Roman half-round tiles, but have almost a double roll to them, being in cross-section like a rather flattened S. They began to appear in the 17th century, as Dutch and Flemish imports, and their use tended to be confined to eastern and north-eastern counties, while plain tiles predominated in the Midlands and south. The exception to this is the Bridgwater pantile from Somerset which had a wide local distribution. Local manufacture began early in the 18th century and a minimum size of 13½ inches by 9½ inches by half an inch thick was laid down by Act of Parliament.

The pantile only overlaps one tile beneath it, but its side joints, the vulnerable part in plain-tiled roofs, are well protected as the ends of the S overlap snugly together. Pantiles can be laid on a relatively low, lightly timbered roof with a pitch of some 30 to 35 degrees, while plain tiles are usually hung on a steeper pitch, of 42½ or 47½ degrees. Many pantiled roofs, however, have steep pitches too, for in areas like East Anglia they were often used as replacements for thatch.

When pantiles were hand-made, variations in shape made it necessary to lay them on a layer of reed or straw and hair mortar. Today it is common to use a couple of layers of bituminous felting beneath them, particularly on low pitch roofs. Because it is difficult to form pantiles around contours they are best used as coverings for simple roof shapes. Normally, of course, they are red-orange in colour, but an interesting development in East Anglia was the black-glazed pantile. The technique of dipping the tiles in a dark glaze probably originated in Holland but it became a speciality of Norfolk manufacturers in the 18th century.

In the later 19th century French and Belgian tiles, flat with interlocking edges, were imported in railway wagons and can be found all over the south-east from Kent to Buckinghamshire.

▧ Slates

Stone roofs, made of flags especially, had the disadvantage of great weight. Slate, found in north and west Wales, in the Lake District, in Leicestershire and in Devon and Cornwall, can be split into much thinner slivers. It is, however, still a heavy material to cart around, so in all but the most expensive houses its use was confined to areas within easy reach of the quarries.

During the second half of the 18th century improvements in transport, notably the development of the canal system, gave slate more widespread popularity. Lake District slate especially was much in demand, particularly in the towns, as a substitute for inflammable thatch. (You can identify some houses that have had their thatch replaced by slate or tiles by the tell-tale marks the earlier, thicker, covering has left higher up the chimney stack.)

Welsh slate really became popular later, with the development of the railways and by the late 19th century it was in use everywhere. The thin blue-grey Welsh slates were riven (split) and cut into pieces of uniform sizes, each size having a colourful and feminine name. Slaters dealt daily with, for example, 'large ladies', 'countesses' and 'queens'. These slates were laid in precise and regular courses. The slates from other areas, such as the Lake District, were thicker and less easy to work, so they came in much more random sizes and produced irregular courses. They were laid, like stone slabs, in diminishing sizes from eaves to ridge.

Slates were hung by nails on wood battens on low-pitched roofs (30 to 35 degrees) and had a lifespan of about a hundred years. Often the cause of failure is the metal nail; if this erodes the slate may slip, long before it is itself badly worn. Ridges were covered with hewn stone pieces, moulded lead or special interlocking slates called 'wrestlers'.

▒ GUTTERING ▒

It is necessary to keep the walls of a house as dry as possible to prevent internal damp and associated evils like mould and other fungal growths. The top of the walls, where the roof ends at the eaves, is especially vulnerable to the rainwater running down, and needs protection.

Thatched roofs present few problems because they are well over-hung and the water drips down a foot or more away from the walls. Early stone, slate and tiled roofs often had good over-hangs too, but a better way of ensuring that the water keeps away from the walls is to catch it in guttering, carry it downwards in a pipe and send it away from the house in a drain. Gutterings are also needed in the valleys of a roof, where two pitches meet at an angle, to speed water away from vulnerable joints, and around the border of a parapet roof.

Wooden box gutters, lined with lead, were used for larger houses, often disguised as classical cornices. Lead was also used to line valleys and the area behind parapets, although because of the cost it was generally reserved for better class houses. Down pipes were also formed in cast lead and had hopper heads, often with decorative castings and dates. Cast iron and zinc were standard from the late 18th century. The former, still in use today, is the longest lasting and soundest of all types of rainwater goods available.

Cast iron gutters and down pipes are the first choice in all repair work to historic and older houses because of their superiority to modern plastic substitutes. Indeed, in repairing old houses, surviving cast iron should be retained and deficiencies made good. While plastic may be suitable for modern housing estates it should be avoided in the traditional construction which is the subject of this book, being a poor substitute for cast iron. Extruded aluminium and other metals have also grown in popularity in recent years and have some of the qualities of cast iron, but with older buildings cast iron is the material of choice.

The Walls

If the basic task of a roof is to keep out the rain, then the primary job for a wall is to keep the wind at bay. Some walls act as supports for the roof and so need strength to take its weight. Others are not load-bearing: if the roof structure is held up by a timber frame, the wall becomes mere in-filling and can be made of comparatively weak material, like wattle and daub.

The early housebuilders built their walls as they did their roofs, with materials that came easily to hand: turf and earth, mud and clay, rubble and stone. Only later, with improving transport and communication, did materials like brick come into widespread use.

▨ TURF ▨

The most primitive form of walling was turf. Close-cropped sods, anything from 2 to 6 inches thick, were cut and laid in courses like brickwork. At their base would be a plinth of rubble, and sometimes loose stones were placed on top as extra support for the roof timbers. Walls could be strengthened at their corners, or along their length, with wooden posts.

▨ CLAY OR MUD ▨

Clay or earth is much more durable. Many thousands of houses built of mud or clay several centuries ago in England are still standing. All a mud house requires, so the country saying goes, is 'a good hat and a good pair of boots' – the 'hat' being a thatch or other form of roof that keeps the rain off and projects it away from the vulnerable wall surface; the 'boots' being dwarf walls of rubble beneath the mud to keep it out of direct contact with the ground, in effect a surprisingly effective damp-proof course.

For proper protection, a mud walled house also needs an 'overcoat' – of render or stucco – which can then be painted, tarred or whitewashed over. The overcoat often disguises the mud walled house. The best clue to recognition is that it will often have rounded edges, both at the house corners and around the doors and windows. The thickness of the walls depends on the quality of the sub soil in the cob area – the better the binder, the thinner the wall. In Devon

95

walls can be several feet thick at the base while in Buckinghamshire 'witchert' cob walls can be less than 18 inches thick in a house.

The mud was mixed with all sorts of other materials: straw to make the goo workable, animal dung as a 'binder', or chalk, pebbles, broken bricks and even broken crockery as added aggregate. If you were lucky, natural clays ideal for walling could be found locally and needed no additive apart from chopped straw. Whatever the materials, though, three well-defined techniques for using them grew up in different parts of the country. One uses a clay and straw mix laid in layers, the best known examples being Devon and Dorset cob or Buckinghamshire 'witchert'. In the second, moulds or shuttering are filled up with rammed earth or clay; and in the third, clay is moulded into blocks for laying like brickwork. These techniques were in use from medieval times right up to the 18th and 19th centuries, although the last two are relatively rare.

▓ Mixed Clay and Straw (Cob)

This was the commonest system and has been particularly used in the south-west (especially Devon), in the Midlands and in the north-west. It was also widespread in Wales, Ireland and Scotland. We will describe the Devon cob method, for the basic techniques are as used elsewhere, with a few local variations.

Loamy earth is the base material, mixed with water into a thick sticky paste. Added to it are a variety of strengtheners: chopped straw or reed, animal dung, chalk, sand, gravel, small pebbles and stones. The glue-like mixture is then laid in layers, varying in thickness according to locality.

People in an area to the south-west of Aylesbury in Buckinghamshire were lucky in having a naturally occurring chalky-clay which, when mixed with straw, proved an excellent walling material. Called witchert, it is stronger than cob, in effect a weak lime concrete, so walls can be thinner. It is still to be found in many old houses in the area.

▓ Earth Walls (Pisé de Terre)

In this walling technique, loose earth was poured between timber or wattle shuttering and rammed in solidly: a less skilled process than cob and allowing any old soil to be used. When set the shuttering was removed. It is much more common on the Continent than in England and tended to be used on landed estates in the late 18th and 19th centuries, with a revival after World War I during a great brick famine.

▓ Clay Lumps or Bats

Clay and straw mixtures were also moulded in wooden frames into large oblong blocks, and allowed naturally to dry out (for up to a month) before being laid in courses like brickwork, with clay mortar between them. Such clay lumps or clay bats were generally confined to East Anglia, the technique having been imported from Germany or Scandinavia.

After being smoothed off, the walls were given a protective rendering of lime-plaster or primitive cement. Colour or whitewash completed them and was applied regularly giving the bright, tidy appearance so characteristic of many English villages with mud-walled houses and cottages.

STONE

As a building material stone has a ancient pedigree. It was used in the earliest houses in the west and north of Britain where the scarcity of trees meant timber construction was not feasible. For their dome-shaped huts our distant ancestors picked stones from the ground, thus clearing their fields for tilling while providing material for shelter. Its capacity to stand the test of time also makes stone a natural choice for monumental architecture, whether in the mysterious circles of Stonehenge, Avebury or elsewhere, or in temple and church, castle and cathedral. Stone buildings are generally only to be found where stone itself abounds. If an alternative is readily available, as timber is in the south-east, it will be used instead. However, it must be remembered that stone came into many areas at house and cottage level only in the 17th century, replacing timber-framing; that is to say, quarried stone became affordable below gentry level. Areas where this can be seen include north Buckinghamshire, Nottinghamshire and Yorkshire.

Britain is fortunate, however, in having a wide choice of stone suitable for building: granites and similar rock, sandstones and limestones, flints and cobbles. All such stones are used, and their different shapes, colours and textures give distinctive regional appearances to the older buildings of our towns and villages.

Geologists classify rocks according to their age and the manner in which they are formed. First, there are primary – or igneous – rocks 'from the fire', formed by the cooling and solidification of molten material from deep beneath the earth's surface. Granite is a prime example. Then there are the secondary – or sedimentary – rocks, made from the disintegrated fragments of other rocks, from dead and decayed organic material, or from chemical precipitation from watery solutions. They are formed in layers, usually originally beneath the sea, and among them are sandstones, limestones and chalk. A third type of rock is the metamorphic, formed by further action on igneous or sedimentary rock by heat or pressure or both. Slate is the most notable building material of this type.

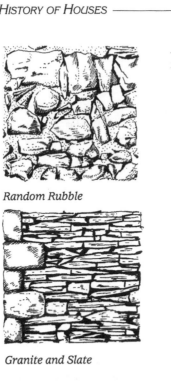

Random Rubble

Coursed Rubble

Granite and Slate

Brick and Flint

Pebble and Brick

Chalk and Sandstone

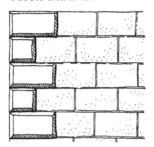

Ashlar Stone

Diagonal Cobbles

▓ Granites

Although in strictly geological terms, 'granite' refers to a well-defined type of rock, as far as the quarryman and the stonemason are concerned, it is a name to be used for a number of igneous rocks used as building stone. Igneous rock varies in colour and texture according to the conditions under which it was formed and what other minerals were amalgamated as the molten raw material (called magma) oozed beneath the earth. It solidified deep beneath the earth's surface but the subsequent weathering away of softer, overlying rock formations has brought it to the surface in many places.

Aberdeen, the granite city, is built of stone in which the crystals are all roughly of the same size, giving the buildings a grey, uniform appearance. English granites, such as those from Devon and Cornwall and from Westmorland, contain larger crystals of felspar, as well as those of the original magma, and so appear more interesting. Felspar can vary in colour from white to various shades of pink, and together with variations in other minerals trapped in the rock it contributes to many local differences in stone colour and texture.

One other igneous rock worth mentioning is tuff, a compacted volcanic ash. There is a deposit of it in the Lake District which gives a very pleasant greenish building stone often seen in the area.

▓ Limestones

While the granites are found in the west – in Devon and Cornwall, Wales and north-west England – further to the east lies a long band of sedimentary rock, much used in building. This limestone belt stretches roughly north-east across the country from Avon and Dorset to the Lincolnshire and Yorkshire coast. Although less hard than granite, limestones are very good for building, being both durable and easier to work. Impurities in the rock mean that it comes in a variety of colours, from the famous mellow yellow of Cotswold stone and the creamy Bath stone of Wiltshire to the brown iron-rich Hornton stone of Warwickshire and north Oxfordshire, the steel-grey Pennine limestone and the greyish or white Portland stone (used in St Paul's Cathedral among many other famous buildings).

▓ Sandstones

Sandstones are also sedimentary rocks, but softer than limestones and formed in a different way. They vary widely in texture from coarse to very fine.

Sandstone is found in various parts of the country, such as Sussex, South Wales, Shropshire and the north-east, but it is particularly prevalent in Derbyshire and West Yorkshire. The Millstone Grit of the South Pennines is perhaps the best known, and is one of the strongest sandstones – but mention should also be made of the New Red sandstone of Cumbria, Lancashire and Cheshire. The Romans used it for constructing Hadrian's Wall, and many buildings in Carlisle and Penrith, for example, contain it. York stone is a very hard and durable sandstone which from early times has found favour for flooring, notably in the Tower of London and other royal palaces, and is still very popular for pavements and road setts.

'Marbles'

Metamorphic rocks – those that have undergone further changes due to heat or pressure, or a combination of both – include marble. True marbles, however, are rare in Britain and most so-called marbles are in fact very hard limestones. English 'marbles', which can be highly polished to resemble the 'real' thing, include Sussex marble and Purbeck marble.

Flints, Cobbles, Pebbles

Flints are irregular nodules of silica found in chalk. Although they are easy enough to dig out (the earliest mines were for flint) their irregular shape causes difficulties in building. They are used, however, in areas where other good walling material is scarce, such as in East Anglia, south and south-eastern England.

Cobbles are the rounded stones that can be picked from river beds or fields, while pebbles are smaller (3 inches across is usually taken as the dividing line) and generally found on the sea-shore. Cobbled walls are particularly to be found in Cumbria and Lancashire and in Humberside, while pebbles are prevalent along the East Anglian, Kent and Sussex coasts.

Building Techniques with Stone

Obviously the best way to build in stone is to cut the rock into uniformly-shaped rectangular blocks, to be laid in courses rather like bricks. Perfectly cut stone (usually sawn) with knife-thin joints is known as 'ashlar', while less perfect hewn stone or rough sawn stone is known as 'rubble'. Ashlar is of course the most expensive way and tended to be used for the finer houses with wealthy owners. The less well-off, however, could put on a show for the world. There are plenty of examples of everyday houses that are apparently of ashlar construction, but when you walk round the house you may find that the side walls are not nearly so well constructed, being made with rough masonry or of brick – and the back wall, hidden from public gaze, will probably be even more crudely put together. The beauty of the facade itself may be only skin deep, with a layer of ashlar backed with rough-hewn rubble masonry to give the wall its strength.

In ordinary houses even the ashlar work was often irregular. Where the courses were of uniform depth, the length of the stones differed; more often than not the courses themselves varied in depth, diminishing towards the eaves. Ashlar, however, is distinguished in having a much smoother finish (dressing) than the hammer-rough blocks of irregular masonry.

Walls made of irregular stone blocks are the commonest in ordinary houses and it required great skills to assemble them into solid and satisfying constructions. The men inducted into these skills, the masons, guarded their methods closely, forming professional bodies or guilds with strict rules of conduct.

There were two types of mason: the hewers or cutters of stone, and those who laid or set it in the wall, although often their tasks intermingled. In the earliest times convenient field stones would be used for walling, but these became increasingly scarce, and the Romans introduced quarrying and cutting techniques. Picks, bars and wedges were the tools of the trade, to split and prise away sections of rock, which were then sawn into blocks prior to final cutting and dressing.

The hewers of stone used mallet and chisel to shape their blocks. This was done at or near the quarry, for all stone is porous to water and when first taken it is wet with 'quarry sap' – a mixture of minerals and water – and most easily cut. Those who worked with 'freestone', that is limestones and fine grained sandstones, became known as freemasons to distinguish them from the 'hard hewers' who worked tougher and more difficult-to-shape stone.

When there is no timber frame in the building to bear the burden of the roof, the builder has to contend not only with the downward stresses but also with the forces that will tend to make the walls bow and buckle outwards. So load bearing walls need strength at right-angles to the surface too, and in the house made of irregular masonry blocks this is usually achieved by making the walls thick and by placing in them frequent bonding or 'through' stones, running right back from the exterior to the interior surface.

The characteristics of the stone will determine the surface pattern of the wall, and this adds to the fascinating regional variations in the appearance of our houses. If the stones are very irregular, the wall may be jointed together in a number of ways. It can be laid without courses, that is with no obvious horizontal joints running along the whole length of the wall, or it may be 'built to courses', with stones selected and joined together so that horizontal strips of mortar are visible. Another alternative is 'snecking', in which there are horizontal joints but they do not run the whole length of the wall. Some local stone, however, like Millstone Grit, could be hewn into such regular blocks that the wall could be laid in courses with almost the same precision as bricks.

With the irregular masonry used in most stone houses, the largest and heav-

101

iest blocks were laid at the bottom of the wall (often large, rounded boulders were used) and the smaller pieces carefully selected and fitted together above them. Any large interior joints would be filled with loose pieces of waste stone, while the horizontal joints were originally packed with earth or clay, and later with lime mortar. Very irregular stones will require wide joints between them and for extra strength small stones were pushed into the mortar, a technique known as 'galletting'.

When the stone was particularly rough and of poor quality the wall would need reinforcing with regular 'lacing' courses of better quality stone or brick. Special attention, too, had to be paid to the corners, or quoins, which were built with superior quality, better finished stones. It was common practice for the corners of a house, and the dressings around doors and windows, to be fitted by skilled craftsmen while the rest of the walling was left to the less experienced men. The unit size of the stones used at quoins and window and door surrounds was larger than that of the rest of the wall, and where the wall was coursed, the courses aligned with those of the dressings.

Any opening in a wall detracts from its strength, so windows in particular tend to be both few and small in houses built of irregular stone pieces, but when good quality, well-cut stone was used skilled masons could produce a range of impressive, and beautiful windows.

Flints, cobbles and pebbles, because of their small size and rounded or irregular shape, presented particular problems for the wall builder. Masses of earth or clay, and later, lime mortar were needed to help with stability. Cobbles were often laid uncoursed while pebbles, smaller and of more uniform size, were usually laid in courses. In some areas naturally occurring pebbles and cobbles were found that were flattened and elongated rather than rounded, and these could be laid in diagonal or herring-bone patterns.

Again, better quality material is needed around door and window openings and, although not absolutely necessary, it is often used at the corners too. In later houses brick was used, and it is found in strengthening lacing courses along the wall too. Brick is also often found in flint walls, both in lacing courses and interspersed with the stones to give pleasing geometrical effects ('chequer boards' are common). Flints can be laid alone, either undressed, split or 'knapped', that is chipped to give a smooth and roughly square end, about 4 inches across. Rounded flints require plenty of mortar at the joints and often galletting for extra strength, while in knapped flint walls the joints are much thinner.

▩ TIMBER FOR WALLS ▩

Walls made mainly of clay, stone or brick can be described as 'mass walling', in that the weight of the roof and any inner floors is taken by the whole mass of the wall. The other technique is to build 'frame walls', where the load is taken by a framework of timbers and the wall itself is merely a non-load bearing infill to keep out the wind and the rain. It may be that if timbers fail, or sag a little, the wall panels will bear some of the load, but that is not what they are designed to do. As described in detail in the chapter on roofs, timber-frame houses are of two main types: cruck frames and box frames. The A-shaped crucks transmit the whole load of the roof to the ground while in the box frame it is supported on a hollow cube of posts and beams. Between these two types are many hybrids.

Construction techniques varied, although both methods required the help of friends and neighbours to manoeuvre the heavy timbers into position. In cruck frame houses, the crucks themselves were first hauled and levered upright and then ridge piece, purlins and wall plates were eased into pre-cut joints and sockets, to complete the rigid structure. Box frames, it seems, were usually built from the ground up: the vertical corner posts first being set in massive ground sills or sole plates, then the longitudinal wall plates and lateral tie beams set into joints at the top of the posts.

Timber houses were almost invariably 'built by numbers': the timbers were squared and jointed by the wrights in their own yards and taken by cart to the house site for erection. To make sure all the beams, posts and joints were assembled correctly, the joints were identified by chiselled or scratched Roman numerals, or by special gouged carpenter's marks, so that each tenon could be mated with its proper mortice. No nails were used in the construction, the whole frame being secured by wooden pegs, generally made of heart of oak.

From the earliest times, oak has been the timber of choice for houses, although other woods, such as elm, chestnut and willow, were used too. Oak and other timber was used 'green' because it is easier to work when new felled, although as it seasons in situ it warps, shrinks and 'shakes' (splits) which gives timber-framed buildings their characteristic distortions. Green elm is particularly prone to warping and shrinkage and by the end of the 18th century elm was used for about half of the barns built.

The infilling between the principal timbers of the frame varies in style around the country. In southern and eastern counties the space between the principals was filled with many vertical posts called studs, usually on the 'show' elevations that everyone would see. After 1600 or so close studding, as this technique is called, waned and panel framing became the norm, that is square panels of infill, perhaps because timber was less plentiful and more costly.

103

Elaborately patterned timber work, known as magpie work, was a common feature of timber-framed houses in the Midlands and particularly in the North West.

In the western part of the country they preferred squarish panels, composed of both vertical and horizontal timbers. Again, as timber became scarcer, the panels increased in size. In some areas, notably Lancashire, Cheshire and the North Midlands, the timbers, often highly decorated in intriguing patterns, were in the 17th century and later blackened with a protective coat of pitch in magnificent contrast to the whitewashed panels. This effect is known as 'magpie' work. Elsewhere in the country the wood and the panels were limewashed, weathering to give the oak a delightful silvery-grey colour in contrast to the white panels.

One striking feature of many 14th to 17th century timber houses is 'jettying', whereby the upper floor overhangs the ground floor, from the French *jeter*, to throw. There are many theories that try to explain the origins and enormous popularity of the jetty. It probably originated in towns where projecting the floor joists for successive storeys increased the floor area. Often rentals were based on ground floor area and in a four or five storey building the top floor could almost double the area of the ground floor.

Clearly in towns space was at a premium and the cantilever effect assisted stability. However, the important thing about jettying is that it shows your neighbours and passers-by that you have a building with an upper storey or storeys. Jetties are almost always only on the show side, rather like close-studding, so it is all about fashion and status. Structurally there is no need for a jetty in the wide open spaces of the countryside, in farmhouses and villages, so fashion is the key. A characteristic hall and cross wing house has each end jettied to the front either side of the hall. In the late 16th century, or whenever the hall was floored over, many owners inserted a central jetty section so that the house then had a continuous jetty: the neighbours now knew the house was all two storeyed.

Some buildings were jettied on more than one side, for example corner houses. Here the joists were jointed into 'dragon' beams running diagonally across the upper floor, so called because their ends were often carved with dragon heads. The corner post supporting the dragon beam also provided an opportunity for carved decoration, such as angels or battlements, as did the bressumer boards which were often attached across the ends of the jetty joists.

The most common way of filling in the panels between the timbers was with wattle and daub. The first step was to insert sprung vertical oak staves, fitted into auger holes in the lower side of the panel's top timber and into a slot in its lower timber, giving an effect like a barred window. Across these were woven supple withies or hazel, basket fashion, and on this wattle framework was then daubed a mixture of clay, dung and horse hair, finished off with a coating of plaster, both inside and out.

Other infilling included small stone slabs, wall tiles and brick. When bricks are used the panels are often, although not always, whitewashed over. Most such 'nogging' is a later replacement for wattle-and-daub (in which case auger holes and slots may still be visible if a panel is removed), but some, particularly in the 17th century, can be original (in which case there will be no auger holes or slots provided). The bricks were not only laid horizontally in standard bonds

The usual way of filling the panels between the timbers of a wall was with wattle and daub. Withies were woven basket fashion on vertical staves to make a frame. This was then daubed with a mixture of clay, dung and horsehair and finished off with a coat of plaster.

105

but vertically and in herringbone. Generally speaking bricks laid horizontally tend to be later replacement for wattle-and-daub while herringbone or thin brick may more likely be 17th century or even earlier.

▓ Cladding Timber Walls

The identification of timber-framed houses might seem to be simple, but although those with exposed timbers are indeed obvious at first sight, the majority of timber houses will not reveal their basic structure to the outside world: they were covered with a variety of claddings. This is particularly true of houses built of poorer quality or second-hand wood. Not only did the covering enhance appearance, it also gave further protection against the weather and against the risk of fire. Walls might simply be rendered over with lime mortar and/or plaster or, from the late 18th century onwards, with cement. Or they could be weatherboarded, a technique much used in eastern and south-eastern England, and especially in Essex and Kent.

Clapboard or weatherboard was used on farm buildings from as early as the 16th century, and on timber-framed church towers from even earlier. But it did not really become popular for homes until the late 18th century and then generally only for smaller houses and cottages, by which time of course the houses were not true timber-framed ones but had light softwood stud frames.

Oak or elm were often used for the earliest weatherboards, pegged in horizontal strips to the internal timbers, but later on deal, which was nailed to the studs, was the usual choice for 18th century cottages. The strips could be butted, but were more often overlapped and frequently rebated along the lower edge. This softwood boarding was always painted or colourwashed (usually white) while for barns and some cottages it was tarred. Oak and elm weatherboards were either left untreated or were tarred.

Weatherboarding in oak or elm was used as early as the 16th century, and most usually along the eastern coasts of Kent, Essex and Sussex. It served both to cover poor structural timbers and to protect the walls from exposure to rain and wind. It became fashionable in the 18th century, and was typically painted white.

Plaster and lath could be used for both internal and external wall covering. Closely spaced laths, usually of split oak, were nailed to the timbers of the frame. Then this was covered with plaster made from lime and sand mixed with cleaned animal hair.

Another cladding technique, from the mid 18th century onwards, was to hang the wall with slates or tiles. In exposed areas especially, elderly panels of wattle and daub were not really effective protectors against the weather, so when clay roofing tiles became more readily available and cheaper, they were quickly adapted for use on walls too. Laths were nailed across the external timbers and the tiles hung on them triple-lap, that is with each tile overlapping two others below. Ordinary roof tiles were commonly used, with special moulded ones to cover jambs and corners, although very pleasant decorative effects were sometimes obtained by using different colours or tiles with shaped bottom edges, producing intricate geometrical patterns. When jettied houses were subsequently tile covered, the jetty was often under built in brick and the ground floor timbers removed to increase the area of the ground floor room.

Also used on walls were mathematical tiles, otherwise known as brick tiles, for their purpose was to imitate the more expensive brick. Shaped to give an outward appearance of rectangular brick sections, or specially moulded for jambs and corners, these too were hung on laths nailed horizontally to the frame timbers. They were introduced around the middle of the 18th century and were much used in the south-east of England until well into the 19th. They were not affected by the Brick Taxes of 1784 to 1850, so town dwellers particularly found that they could give their homes a fashionable brick built appearance without going to the expense of the real thing. Further imitations of stone dressings at doors and windows, made from painted wood or plaster, added to the deception. Mathematical tiles were usually reddish-brown or orange-red, but there are examples of yellows, greys, blacks and even black glazed ones.

Slates, cut small and nailed to laths, were also used in the south-west of

England as a protective covering for timber-frame walls, for example at Totnes, and in the Lake District and North Wales as an extra skin on stone walls, especially at exposed gable ends.

▦ RENDERING ▦

Rendering, the outer coat of plaster or cement, serves two purposes: it adds to the wall's weatherproofing properties and it can have a pleasing decorative effect. It is, of course, particularly suitable for walls of rough stone, but many timber-framed houses were also sheathed with an outer skin of plaster. The most popular early method was to mix clay with cow dung to make it more workable, and with animal hair for strength, and to spread the mixture evenly across the wall. In the west of England Wet Dash was a common alternative: a gooey mixture was literally thrown at the wall. Such rendering sticks better, but gives a rougher finish. Walls were then given a final coating of limewash (either white or coloured) which was renewed at regular intervals.

In the 13th century, plaster of paris was introduced and because of its brilliant whiteness it was used for a time as an external rendering. Its expense, however, meant that it was soon used only for interior walls.

Rendering really came into its own in the late 16th and 17th centuries with the use of lime plaster on a base of laths. It has been suggested that the technique became popular as a way of hiding away the scantiness of the timbers by then being used in house-building. But plasterwork was used often on substantially-built early timber-frame houses, particularly in East Anglia, and its main purpose must have been weather-proofing rather than disguise, though no doubt fashion played its part.

The closely spaced laths, usually of split oak, were nailed horizontally to the studs and other timbers in the frame and then covered with a couple of coats of plaster. This was made from lime and sand, mixed with fine cleaned horse or cow hair and beaten to a smooth consistency. The finishing touch was a coat of whitewash or colourwash. The eastern counties are especially rich in plastered and colourwashed houses and cottages which, under steeply pitched roofs, still grace many villages.

The plaster was not always left smooth. In many cases it had patterns inscribed on the surface, or was moulded into a variety of designs known collectively as pargetting (from the French *par* – all over; *jeter* – to throw). Such decorative mouldings were in use in the late 16th century but were at their most popular in the 17th and early 18th centuries, again especially in the rich eastern counties. By the mid-18th century, however, fashion again favoured plain-plastered walls, both in new timber-frame houses and in renovated old ones,

Above: *Seventeenth century pattern of moulded pargetting.*

Left: *Fan combed pargetting.*

although pargetting enjoyed something of a comeback in the late 19th century and elaborate plaster mouldings are still in use today. (For an example of a rendered pargetted house see p 25.)

The return to plain plastering coincided with the use of strong, smooth stucco as a rendering on buildings of stone or brick. The works of Palladio, the great Italian architect, were having a profound effect on British architecture in the 18th century. Not only were Palladian designs copied, but also the technique of putting a smooth rendering over all the rough stone and brick work, so that the eye can appreciate the building as a whole and not be distracted by joints and mortar. It is often difficult to distinguish houses built of stone and rubble and stuccoed over from those with timber frames covered with lath and plaster. The best clues come at door and window openings, where the reveals in timber-framed constructions are generally shallower. In the 18th century, too, the quality of renderings was much improved with the introduction of cements which were both easier to work and gave a more durable finish. The stucco was often incised with lines to imitate the blocks in coursed ashlar masonry.

Portland cement was introduced in 1824 and has remained to this day the basis for most renderings. Its greyish colour, however, is not particularly attractive and one way of disguising it was to pebble-dash the walls, throwing pebbles at the surface while the rendering was still wet. White cement, which helps overcome the problem, was not introduced until the 1930s.

At first cement renderings were left unpainted but later were either colourwashed or covered with oil-based paints which are more easily cleaned.

109

▨ THE COLOUR OF THE WALLS ▨

Through the centuries white has been by far the most popular colour for the walls of houses. It still is today: although a wide range of colours is now available, white still accounts for something like half of the sales of exterior paints and finishes.

In times past almost every dwelling, from country cottage to castle keep, was whitewashed (like the White Tower, the keep of the Tower of London, its white coating long since washed away). Based on ground chalk or kilned lime steeped in water, limewash also had a binding material added, traditionally skimmed milk or tallow, to help stop the whitewash oozing away in heavy rain.

Such whitewashes, however, have only a limited lifespan and fresh coats need to be applied every year or two, and in time a good thick layer of protective lime can be built up. Being porous it should always be used for old buildings as their walls need to 'breathe', that is let moisture from within out and absorb moisture from outside. Modern cement-based paints stop this 'breathing' and may be alright for modern cavity wall houses where the fundamentals of design are different, but not for older houses. A modern house presents a series of layers to resist water: an outer skin, usually of brick; a cavity, now filled with insulation material; and an inner skin, usually of blockwork. Coating the outside skin with non-porous (nowadays often described as 'micro porous', whatever that means) cement-based paints is thus acceptable, but traditional construction depends on the ability of the wall to absorb moisture into its inner third and 'exhale' or evaporate it out again. Interfere with this fundamental and decay will occur as sure as eggs are eggs.

In the past, owners of more humble homes often did not bother to paint the whole of their house. Perhaps only the front wall would be whitened or even just the surround to the door. Not everyone stuck to plain white: colours were introduced to make the more important houses and fortifications stand out from the crowd. In some areas a strong tradition of colour-washed houses grew – Suffolk Pink being a case in point, for which bull's blood was added to the limewash. Soot and charcoal were other early colouring materials as was the root of the madder plant, or rose madder. Various minerals were also used: red cinnabar (mercuric sulphide), red and yellow ochres (ferric oxides), minium (red lead) and verdet (from verdigris, the green discolouring of copper). Later pigments used iron and manganese, and the brown earth, umber, which could be heated to give the deeper colour of burnt umber. Generally speaking, earth and blood additives were those used for cottages, it being cheap and easy to produce such colours as ochres, dark reds, browns and pinks. The range of colours using the more expensive pigments appeared higher up the social scale.

Complex and jealously-guarded formulae also gave medieval painters whites and yellows from lead-based pigments; vermilion from sulphur and quicksilver; blue from cobalt; and a variety of other hues using, for instance, the oxides of antimony and tin. Medieval paints with metallic bases could be downright dangerous and colours were often unstable due to chemical interaction of pigments with the lime. This was not too much of a problem, however, because repainting was done so regularly. The 18th and 19th centuries saw the introduction of further colours – especially fresh blues, greens and yellows – and cheaper production of bright-coloured paints. Yet further pigments became available as a result of the revolution in applied organic chemistry in the late 19th and early 20th centuries, leading to a colour spectrum today of almost infinite variety.

When stucco became popular in the late 18th century it was usual either to mix-in pigments with the rendering, or to limewash it to imitate natural stone colours. But increasing air pollution in our towns led to a switch to oil-based paints which were easy to clean. Cream was a popular colour for stucco since it was nearest in colour to the fashionable Bath stone.

Oil paint had in fact been known as early as the 13th century but because of its expense, was seldom used for house exteriors. When high quality wood, notably fine oak, was used for house-building there was no need to protect it, nor disguise it with paint, although a covering of varnish, oil or beeswax and turpentine was often applied to doors to protect against scuffing and marking. However, there was also a tradition of painting timber-framed buildings in a variety of rich, if not gaudy to the modern eye, colours. A good example of a 16th century timber-framed Tudor inn fully restored to its original, somewhat shocking colour scheme is the Queen's Head in the Market Square at Newark in Nottinghamshire.

With the introduction of softwoods such as pine and deal, protection was necessary and white lead-based paints were commonly used, as other shades tended rapidly to discolour and fade. By the late 18th century a variety of longer-lasting oil paints for woodwork were introduced and often houses were painted in soft and subtle shades. But again the pollution of the air by industry forced the 19th century householder to search for more practical colours and black and ochre were popular early in the century, with chocolate browns (especially for windows) and dark greens and blues coming into vogue a little later.

Today's paints, in their wide range of colours, are mixed with a variety of modern materials such as polyurethane, for a tough and lasting finish. For rendered masonry and brick walls, coloured cements and cement-based and textured resin-based paints have, unfortunately and ill-advisedly, largely replaced the traditional lime washes.

It is pleasing to revive and retain local colours and if you want to check on your local traditions the council Conservation Officer should be able to help.

111

Black and white contrasts find particular favour in western districts; cottages and farms with white walls and black-painted quoins, windows and doors are common. It is interesting to note that while in Essex and Hertfordshire weatherboarded houses were usually painted black (they were originally tarred), in Kent, white is the traditional weatherboard colour. In other areas, notably East Anglia, strong colours like pinks and reds are often favoured.

▨ BRICK FOR WALLS ▨

Shaped, baked clay bricks have been used for building walls since the earliest times but they did not become popular for ordinary English houses until the 15th century, and it was not until the 19th that they were a universal building material. The Romans brought a superior skill in brickmaking to Britain, but even so, it is rare to find Roman houses built solely of brick. Brick bonding courses, arches, and floor supporting pillars are more common. Roman bricks were in general thin and perhaps the description 'wall tile' is more suitable than 'brick'. When the Roman occupation ended, however, the craft of brickmaking was neglected, although the bricks themselves were highly prized and Roman buildings were plundered for them to use in new buildings, particularly to strengthen corners.

Similarly following the Norman conquest Roman ruins were pillaged for bricks for use in churches, military buildings and the fortified castles and keeps of the rich and powerful. The Normans imported large quantities of brick from the Continent but later the home industry was revived, the first English bricks being manufactured around 1200. Unlike Roman 'wall tiles' these bricks were larger and thicker: some $1^3/4$ to $2^3/4$ inches thick and 12 by 6 inches across. Known as 'great bricks' they were made by hand and were often irregular, both in size and shape – and again were seldom used in ordinary homes, not least because of their expense. In the 13th century Flemish craftsmen began to settle in East Anglia and soon introduced their brickmaking techniques there. Flemish bricks were somewhat smaller than the great bricks – some 8 to $9^1/2$ inches long, $3^3/4$ to $4^3/4$ inches wide, and ranging in depth from $1^3/4$ to $2^1/2$ inches. Because they could be held more easily in a man's hand, they could be laid more speedily.

Bricks coming from any particular mould should have been of fairly uniform size but there were in fact quite considerable variations due to the temptation not to fill the mould right to the top. This was because bricks were sold in those days by number, rather than by weight, so there was more profit to be made by using less clay. To discourage such practices the size of bricks was regulated by law in 1571, the so-called 'statute brick' being of the harmonious proportions of 9 inches by $4^1/2$ inches and $2^1/4$ inches deep.

In the 16th and 17th centuries, with England's increasing mercantile prosperity, there was a great rebuilding and, encouraged by increasing scarcity of timber, building with bricks became increasingly popular and widespread. Initially at farmhouse and cottage level this was restricted to chimney stacks. By the end of the 17th century, they had become fashionable for public buildings (Wren's Royal Hospital at Chelsea is a fine example), and the fashion spread to humbler dwellings. Not only were new houses constructed of bricks, but older timber-frame houses, for instance, might be completely encased in a new skin of brickwork, or a false front wall might be built of bricks. Brick nogging was increasingly used to replace wattle and daub as an infilling between wooden frames: a cheaper method of up-dating.

Brick building continued to increase in popularity despite the imposition of a series of brick taxes between 1784 and 1850. The earliest of these taxed bricks by number rather than by size, which encouraged a temporary increase in brick dimensions. Even though length and breadth were fairly well standardised, thickness grew to as much as $3\frac{1}{4}$ inches. (Incidentally, bricks in the North of England are still traditionally somewhat larger than those in the South.) The brick taxes, however, did encourage the development of tax-free alternatives such as timber stud and weatherboarded houses in the south-east, tile hanging and the use of imitation-brick mathematical tiles.

Although increasing quantities of bricks were being made from the 13th century onwards, their early use for everyday houses was confined almost exclusively to the areas where suitable clays were readily available. As with stone, long distance transportation was impractical before the advent of the canals and the railways. Half of the houses built in brick between the 13th century and the late 17th are in East Anglia, where a familiarity with Continental techniques and local shortage of stone also helped brick's popularity.

The early brickmakers were itinerant craftsmen, moving from place to place making and laying their bricks: they were skilled in both arts. Near many villages a brickfield may still be found, usually now an area of bumpy ground from which clays had been dug out. And by many a country house or farm you will find the pond that was originally a clay pit. Bricks were fired in clamps on site – and those at the centre had the best firing. They were used as facing bricks while less well-baked ones were built into interior walls. By 1800 virtually every town and village had at least one brick pit, sometimes several, and these only declined after 1900 when mass produced brick made them uneconomic.

By the end of the 17th century good quality brickmaking was helped by the invention of the pugmill which mixed clays to an even consistency. By the time the brick taxes were abolished, in the 19th century, brickmaking had advanced from a craft to very big business, using all the mass-production techniques brought in by the Industrial Revolution.

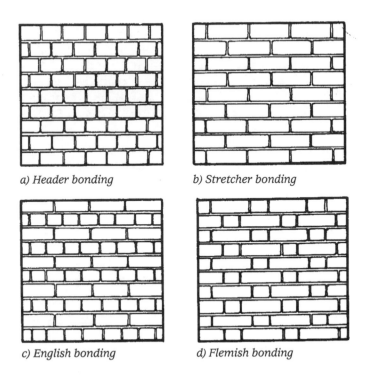

a) Header bonding   b) Stretcher bonding

c) English bonding   d) Flemish bonding

▓ Bricklaying styles and colours

The earliest bricks were of irregular shape and size and although laid in courses showed no regular pattern or 'bond'. Later, however, a number of distinct styles emerged. In English Bond, for instance, there are alternate courses of headers (bricks laid so that their head, or end, shows) and stretchers (laid longways on). In Flemish Bond, introduced in the 17th century, there were alternate headers and stretchers in each course. There were many variations of these basic bonds, among them English Garden Wall Bond, where three or five courses of stretchers alternated with one course of headers; and Flemish Garden Wall Bond, where there were three stretchers to each header in every course. Other bonds, with their individual patterns, include Monk Bond, Rat-trap Bond, English Cross Bond and Header Bond, where each course is composed solely of headers, an arrangement favoured for decorative work. Today the most common arrangement is Stretcher Bond, every course consisting only of stretchers. This is because of the widespread use of cavity walling, in which there are two separate 'skins' of wall, each of only a single brick width. This method had long been used for brick nogging panels in timber-framing but only for very humble houses at the beginning of the 19th century.

114

This type of herringbone decorative brickwork was often used as an infill between timber panels, known as nogging.

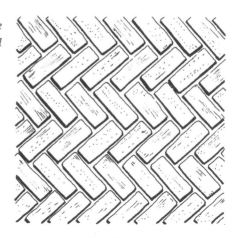

Although most bricks have always been some shade of red, variation in the composition of clays from one locality to another has led to some striking colour differences, a variety further enhanced by the techniques of firing and the use of additives, like sand. Basically it is iron that gives bricks their red colour, and in Lancashire where the clay has a high iron content they can be almost scarlet in appearance. But if hard iron-bearing clays, such as those in Staffordshire, are fired to very high temperatures, they can turn blue or purple. Other notable regional variations, due to the presence of different minerals in the clay, include blacks from Surrey, Sussex, Berkshire and South Wales, browns from Humberside, greys from Oxfordshire, Berkshire and Hampshire, yellows from the Thames Valley, and whites in Sussex and East Anglia.

Individual variations in any batch of bricks meant that old walls have marvellously subtle shadings of colour, but the bricklayer was able also to exploit more marked colour differences by laying bricks in decorative geometric patterns. Some bricks for this were produced in special firings: a vitrified metallic purple was a popular choice. Decorative brickwork was much favoured in the Middle Ages and under the Tudors, but later, when stucco became fashionable, the craft was neglected. It enjoyed a spectacular revival in Victorian times when new technologies produced bricks in a wide range of colours and a variety of finishes, particularly vitreous glazes, which architects were quick to exploit: a style known as 'constructional polychromy'.

Further decorative effects could be achieved by using moulded, carved and rubbed bricks, both to produce imitations of classical forms and in marvellously intricate designs formed in the finely ground high quality brick earths. Terracotta, a very finely ground refined material for bricks, was particularly suitable for mouldings. Although it had been introduced in the early 16th century its use was short lived until a revival in the 18th, and again in the late 19th

115

DIAPER WORK: *decorative geometric patterns of different coloured bricks were first used in late medieval and Tudor times. With later advances in technology and mass produced bricks it really found favour in Victorian house building.*

century. A splendid example of a public building with extensive use of terracotta is London's Natural History Museum.

Even when brick was not used for whole walls, it found favour for dressings of quoins, window and door surrounds, while the rest of the wall might be, for instance, in irregular rubble stone or flint. Conversely, in areas where there was a strong tradition of stone building, bricks might be used for general walling while quoins, windows and doors were dressed with good masonry blocks. And many houses that were built of timber, and even of stone, would have brick chimneys, because of the ease of building and brick's fire-resistant properties.

▧ INTERIOR WALLS ▧

Inside the house the walls have been given a variety of treatments over the years, ranging from the plain and simple of earlier ordinary homes to the elegant and fancy of Georgian and Victorian mansions.

In early timber-framed houses, when good oak was in plentiful supply, the wall beams and studs were left exposed, with the space between them filled with wattle and daub, plastered over and coated with a limewash which was usually white but could be coloured. Sometimes the walls and timbers were painted to represent panelling or leather hangings, sometimes the timbers were picked out differently from the plastered wattle and daub or garnished with improving texts in what is known, around 1600, as 'black letter' style. By 1700 all but the major structural timbers were concealed by lath and plaster or by painted softwood panelling. This too was the normal procedure with mass walls of stone, cob, clay lump or brick.

In Tudor, Elizabethan and Jacobean times, particularly in the larger and finer houses, wood panelling was often fixed to the walls, not only to produce a mellow and elegant interior, but to provide insulation as well. The panelling, usually in oak and often finely carved, might extend to the full height of the room, or be perhaps just waist high. It is easily recognisable, being in small square or rectangular panels set in framing. If softwood was used it was always painted: the

116

Wood panelling provided warmth and insulation to a room, while protecting the plaster walls from damage. It was prevalent in Tudor and Jacobean times, but fell from favour with the introduction of wallpaper in the mid-18th century. The example shown here is of a particularly fine Tudor type known for obvious reasons as 'linen fold' panelling.

current fad for stripping pine doors and panelling has no basis in historical practice.

The lower third of the wall is known as the dado and its panelling was protected from damage by the backs of chairs – which were replacing stools and benches – by a protruding chair or dado rail. Panelling, particularly half-panelling, was still popular in the early Georgian period but fell from fashion in the mid-18th century when wallpaper became the vogue.

Windows

Windows are among the most important features of a house, adding much to its character. They are its 'eyes'; without windows the walls are blank and blind.

The well lit and well ventilated houses of today with their large glazed windows are vastly different from earlier homes. The earliest peasant houses often had no windows at all, such light and air as did penetrate their gloomy and smoke-filled interiors coming from the single door opening. Even when windows were introduced, they were small and draughty affairs, their main job being to ventilate rather than to let in light. The word window comes from the old Norse *windauga* or 'wind-eye', although the Saxons used to call them *windi-durs* or 'wind-doors'.

As well as letting out some of the smoke these narrow holes let in the chill and damp, so they would be covered at night with wooden shutters or with animal skins, to give some protection as the fire burned low. To keep out birds and other intruders, a criss-cross lattice of withies would be built across them, or vertical bars, called mullions, fitted in.

Although the Romans were able to make glass – and did so in Britain – its use in the ordinary post-Roman house is a comparatively modern luxury. Glazed windows were used in many buildings by the third century AD, and fragments of window glass are found on many domestic sites of that date. In the post-Roman period glazed windows in ordinary houses were uncommon until the 17th century. Before that the owner of a small house or cottage had to be content with cheaper alternatives like oiled paper or fabric, or even the stretched placenta of cattle or horses: a mare's placenta was much prized as a window covering by the Irish since it was said to be dagger-proof. The King's excise, too, with heavy taxes and duties on windows and on glass, robbed the common man for many years of the light and ventilation he deserved.

▨ GLASS MAKING FOR WINDOWS ▨

There was no glass making industry in Britain for many centuries after the Romans left. Such glass as was used, in churches and for some of the more important secular buildings, was imported from the Continent. The Normans, for instance, brought their glass across from France, and also imported it from Flanders and Germany.

Glass making started up again here at the beginning of the 13th century, in a small way in a handful of areas which had suitable sands: initially in the Weald of Sussex, Kent and Surrey before spreading elsewhere, for instance, to Shropshire and Cheshire. However, English-made glass remained inferior to the Continental which continued to be imported. In Tudor times Flemish and French immigrants brought with them the skills to produce high quality glass to match the imports.

During the Middle Ages the highly mobile nobility often carried their window glass in wooden or metal frames around in their baggage train, to be installed when they reached one of their many houses. By Tudor times, the larger houses were usually glazed, including the timber framed ones, but glass windows were so highly prized that a house owner would often take them with him when he moved and it was not uncommon for windows to be bequeathed in wills. A law of 1579, however, decreed that glass fixed in windows could not be taken away, 'for without glass is no perfect house'.

Although the Romans had perfected techniques for making reasonably large sheets of window glass, most medieval glass came in small pieces of varying thicknesses which were jointed together with a lattice of lead strips.

The commonest technique for making glass was the crown or Normandy method. After a thick glass 'balloon' had been blown, an iron rod or 'punty' was stuck to it opposite the blow-pipe. Then the blow-pipe, together with an area of glass around it, was removed and the resultant thick vase of glass reheated and spun very rapidly on the punty to provide a flattish disc up to six feet across. The punty was broken away leaving a crown or 'bullion' in the centre. The circular sheet was then cut into square or diamond shaped pieces, called 'quarries', with an average size of about 12 square inches. Panes of crown glass are easily recognised by the curving sweep of the air bubbles trapped within them.

Incidentally the bullion, or bull's eye, now so eagerly sought after as antique 'bottle glass', was regarded as inferior and it was used only in less important windows or in shop-fronts. The lead strips into which the glass panes were set are known as cames or calms. Until the 18th century the quarries were set diagonally in the cames. There are practical aspects to the use of a diamond pattern: the rain water runs more easily off the cames and, more importantly, you can cut more diamond-shaped panes than square ones from a disc of crown glass.

Another, but far less common, technique was to produce *brodeglas* or broad glass. A long cylinder was blown, its ends removed and a cut made along its length so the cylinder could be flattened out into a rectangular sheet.

Towards the end of the 17th century, major changes in architectural fashion

119

led to the increasing popularity of the sash window. This meant a switch from leaded lights to wooden glazing bars, more able to take the strain of opening and closing. Larger panes of glass were also becoming available, imported at first from France, but later made in England, notably in the Newcastle area, and by the middle of the 18th century even small houses had sash windows. As the style progressed, and became more and more refined, the wooden glazing bars became thinner and thinner and by the early 19th century they were sometimes replaced by narrow strips of iron supporting the glass.

The use of glass, however, was sharply constrained in poorer dwellings by a series of Government taxes and excise levies. The levy on glass itself was first imposed in 1695 and it continued with the occasional let up for 150 years. In the early 1800s it could amount to as much as twice the actual production cost of the glass itself (rather like petrol today). Even more damaging to the development of light and airy houses was the notorious window tax, also introduced at the end of the 17th century, and not repealed until 1851. The amount of tax paid depended on the number of windows in the house, and between 1746 and 1808 window taxes were increased six times. The Treasury's coffers may have been swelled, but the levies and taxes kept the less well-off in continuing dark and ill-ventilated houses. Often they could not afford to replace the glass in the few windows they did have, and blocked the holes with rags or paper.

While it is true that some home owners bricked up a few of their windows to avoid paying the tax, the blocked windows often to be seen in old houses are rarely the result of this. Sometimes architects would incorporate dummy windows merely to preserve the symmetry of design, and in other cases a rearrangement of the house's internal features – with perhaps a new staircase or passageway – led to the closing of some original windows.

The aristocracy and the gentry, who set the fashions in architecture, continued to demand bigger and bigger windows for their houses during the 18th century. The size of each pane of glass was, however, still constrained by production techniques: crown glass window panes could seldom be satisfactorily made much bigger than 10 inches across.

Although plate glass, rolled into larger panels, was first produced at St. Helens in Lancashire in 1773 it was not until the abolition of taxes and duties in the mid-19th century that it began to come into widespread use. But once cheap, good quality plate glass was available, there was no stopping it. Glazing bars could be dispensed with, the whole window area being replaced with glass. Whilst this undoubtedly meant that more light was let into the house, windows became less aesthetically pleasing, losing the pattern and proportion of glazing bars or lead cames.

▧ FRAMES FOR WINDOWS ▧

The earliest windows were little more than holes in the wall, designed for ventilation. The Romans did bring with them more sophisticated techniques, including semi-circular arched windows. With the Dark Ages, however, most of the techniques of the Romans were lost and it was not until the conversion of the country to Christianity, and the beginnings of church building, that architecture again revived.

The Anglo-Saxons built principally in wood so few traces of their secular buildings remain, but in the survivors of their stone churches we can find clues to the methods they used to frame their windows. Those Anglo-Saxon buildings that survive are the small churches, the greater having all gone, either having been totally replaced or demolished over the centuries, so we get a distorted and partial view but it seems that Anglo-Saxon church windows were often based on half-forgotten Roman techniques.

The true stone arch was reserved for the wider openings such as tower and chancel arches in parish churches: for larger churches and monasteries proper turned arches were the norm. In what survives the Anglo-Saxon builder often mimicked an arch for his small windows by cutting their solid stone lintels with arch recesses to the underside. In other Anglo-Saxon church windows there were merely two stones leaning against each other, resting on the sill to produce a triangular opening; or even more basic, a solid stone slab pierced with a small circular hole.

Anglo-Saxon windows are all small, due not just to a lack of technical skill, but also occasionally to defensive needs and because the desire was not primarily for internal light but for ventilation. In side walls they were placed high up to reduce draughts and in wooden halls and barns the Anglo-Saxons usually placed their windows at the gable ends (the roofs coming too low at the eaves to allow windows in the side walls). A stone slab with a small hole bored through might be used to close the opening, or a slab of timber 2 or 3 inches thick, perforated with a series of holes and fitted centrally into the width of the wall.

Shutters would also be used. At first they were probably removable and merely pushed into the opening at night, but the Anglo-Saxons also used the method of hanging a swinging shutter on a pivot or harr which slotted into the sill and the lintel. In a basically glass-less society such window openings and shutters were necessary, but in them we can see the beginnings of the windows of today. The pierced stone slab showed an early form of the masonic skill that was to develop into the elegant tracery of the Gothic period; the hinged oak shutter, often perforated, can be seen as a first step towards the side-hung casement window.

By the late Anglo-Saxon period, small arched windows were being built in

121

In the Norman period new building techniques enabled the arched window to develop.

Early Gothic windows were tall and thin. The style developed into double and triple windows, culminating in the delicate tracery and elaborate patterns of the Decorated style. During the Gothic Revival of Victorian times, Gothic style windows were once again favoured.

churches, and double arches developed, the centre being supported on a stone column. The Normans had similar styles but were more accomplished builders in stone and could span much wider apertures, using arches composed of numerous cut stones or *voussoirs*. They used stone, too, in their secular buildings, in their halls and manor houses, and here windows were in the same style as those of their churches, for there was no real division between church and domestic architecture.

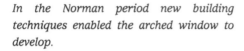 Gothic Windows

The 13th century saw the beginning of Gothic architecture, and the replacement of the rounded Romanesque arch by a pointed one, as used in the great cathedrals. Early Gothic windows were tall and thin, and when larger lights were needed the 'lancets' would be grouped in twos or threes. As the style progressed a further arch was added to surround such groups and the stonework became more intricate, culminating in the delicate tracery and elaborate patterns of the Decorated style. Again the castles and the larger houses followed the fashions of church architecture, but for the ordinary man's home there was little change:

122

the cottage still had a hole in the roof for a chimney and a small unglazed opening for a window. Some shutters, however, were now 'top-hung' and held open by a prop during the day, or made to slide sideways in grooves.

The Decorated style gradually gave way to the Perpendicular in the 15th century, with tall, wide church windows with slender mullions and numerous lights which were often divided by thin horizontal transoms as well. The halls and manor houses had by now lost their fortified character and they adopted and adapted the ecclesiastical styles. Bay windows also made their appearance, as did oriels, many-sided windows jutting out, usually from an upper storey, as at The Old Hall in Gainsborough, Lincolnshire.

In hall houses and other timber-framed houses what we know as 'church tracery' can be found inserted into window openings decked out with cusps and arches, usually cut out of a single sheet of oak, exactly the same way as in the oak chancel screens that survive in so many parish churches. Once again, in timber building there was no real distinction between secular and church building styles.

Casement Windows

The 15th century, too, saw a wider introduction of the iron casement window: a frame of wrought iron, hinged at the side, and glazed with small panes jointed with lead cames. There were vertical and horizontal reinforcing rods for added strength and the leaded lights were wired to these for support. The casement was the prototype of the modern window, but again it should be emphasised that its use was limited to the great houses, manors and halls and to the town houses of the new breed of wealthy merchants. Many were hinged onto spikes set into the stone or timber window frame so the glazed casements could be removed when necessary, sometimes being replaced by solid timber shutters when the owner was away from home.

Fresh air was not much valued in the Middle Ages. On the contrary it was believed that the wind, particularly from the south, brought pestilence with it – a suspicion confirmed in many people's mind by the Black Death of the mid-14th century, which apparently arrived in Dorset from France and spread rapidly up through the country, ultimately killing about one third of the entire population. Wherever possible houses were aligned north/south (often even if the village street ran east/west) so their narrow and windowless ends faced the dreaded south wind.

In Tudor times much more attention was being paid to domestic architecture. In the brick-built houses of this period the windows were set in stone surrounds, with stone mullions and transoms (or moulded brick plastered to look like stone in Essex and other poor stone areas). Similarly windows in the best

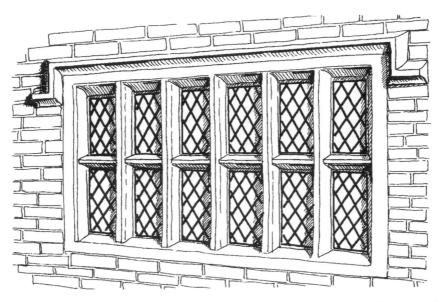

During the great rebuilding of the 16th century mullioned windows, set in stone or iron frames, were fashionable and continued to be widely used up until the 18th century. The small glass panes were usually joined together with lead cames into the familiar diamond pattern.

timber-framed houses tended to reflect in wood the architectural styles of the stonemasons, with mullions copying stone mouldings. In the smaller houses and cottages, however, windows remained simple affairs with the horizontal timbers, the lintel and the sill jointed into the vertical studs of the wall.

The opening was often protected by thin vertical mullions, acting as 'burglar bars', square or diamond-shaped in section. By setting the mullions diagonally at 45 degrees to the window frame face draughts were considerably reduced, the breeze having been concentrated on the way in and dispersed once past the narrow mid point. Visitors to the Weald and Downland Museum, near Chichester, are always amazed at how little draught comes through these diagonal mullion windows.

Shutters were still the rule rather than the exception, either hinged or sliding in grooves. It seems likely that the movable, glazed, wooden-frame window developed as a replacement of the grooved shutter; and as we have seen, these were regarded more or less as items of furniture, to be taken away on moving house, rather than fixtures and fittings. A few of the shutters or glazed frames may have slid vertically. In 1519, for example, a William Horman wrote: 'I have many pretty wyndowes shette with leuys [leaves] goynge up and downe'. This is one of the earliest known English references to a vertical sash-type arrangement, a style for windows that was to gain widespread popularity in the 17th and 18th centuries, although it is clear from other comments by Horman that he is referring to solid timber shutters, rather than glazed ones.

While we can chart the introduction of new styles and developments in windows, it should be remembered that the old styles continued to be used for centuries in the smaller houses and cottages. The forms of windows introduced in medieval times – either a series of thin arched windows, or a squared-off timber frame divided by mullions – continued in use until the end of the 17th century. What is known as the 'sub-medieval phase', a transition between the older series of narrow mullioned 'lights' and the tall, well-proportioned sash window, lasted well into the 18th century in smaller houses, and was still being used for buildings like workshops in the mid-19th century.

'Sub-medieval' windows were much squarer in outline than earlier ones. When the window was in stone it was usually divided in two by a thin mullion, although this was often removed at a later date when new window frames were put in. In brick, windows would have a shallow arch on top and the space was divided into two, or sometimes three, lights by slender wooden mullions. Alternatively the whole window might be divided into rectangular sections with horizontal and vertical glazing bars.

In timber-frame houses, as less wood began to be used in the walls, windows became independent of the wall timbers, having their own jambs instead of the lintels and sills being slotted into the vertical stud work.

The design of mullions changed over the years, the ones made in wood generally reflecting the styles of stone but sometimes lighter in section. The commonest type had plain chamfers, but these were superseded in the later 16th century by splays with a hollowed out section (concave), giving a much lighter effect. In the late 16th century ovolo mouldings became popular. These had a convex shape, with square fillets.

Windows that opened, at least in part, were becoming commoner by the 16th and 17th centuries, with side-hung casements in iron or wood making up one half of the squarish opening.

By the 17th century the influence of the Renaissance was beginning to be seen in domestic architecture, and its classical lines were reflected in the windows which, from being squarish, now became taller rectangles. The mullion and transom were often arranged in the form of a cross, so that the upper lights were smaller than the lower ones, usually twice as high as the upper ones. The glass pieces were still jointed together with lead cames but the traditional diagonal pattern of these gave way to a rectangular one, more in keeping with the lines of the window frame and surrounds.

125

▨ Sash Windows

Perhaps the greatest revolution of all in window design came in the early 1670s with the invention of the counter-weighted timber vertical sliding sash. The vertical sliding window in which the bottom half slid behind a fixed upper half light was known in France and Holland in the earlier 17th century but these were kept open by means of pegs inserted in holes in the window frame. However, it was in England that the true sash window was perfected, probably in the royal Office of Works where lead counter-weights, pulleys and cords were borrowed from clock pendulum technology to produce a window that would hold open in any position. In the earliest sashes of the 1670s and 1680s the upper half of the window was usually fixed, with only the lower section counter-weighted and sliding up and down. Later both upper and lower sections were movable and smooth opening and closing was ensured by the system of pulleys and counter-weights hidden within the window frame.

The word sash is of French origin, from *chassis* which means a frame, but it is interesting that the English-speaking world seized on the counter-balanced sliding sash window and they spread wherever the British settled, including through what is now the United States, the West Indies, Australia and in every corner of the former British Empire. Holidaymakers in Minorca may be surprised to see them in Port Mahon and elsewhere: a legacy of British rule in the 18th century. Elsewhere the sash window did not catch on and the casement window is near universal.

The double-hung vertical sliding sash with counterweights was a revolution in window design in the late 17th century. In this example from the mid-18th century you can see the internal shutters folded back into the reveals.

In earlier sash windows the wooden frames were usually fitted flush with the wall's outer surface, but wooden windows were considered a great fire hazard, especially in towns, and the London Building Acts in 1707 and 1709 required that they be set back four inches from the face of the wall. This style was adopted in some other places too, although in many areas the sash box frame remained flush with the wall face. Another trend in design was towards more and more slender and delicate glazing bars; by the beginning of the 19th century they had become very thin indeed.

The tall rectangular window remained popular throughout all the changes in design of the English house: in classic Georgian windows and through the Greek and Gothic revivals of the 18th and 19th centuries. There were variations in style, of course, such as the elegant 'Palladian' or 'Venetian' window which gave more light to staircase landings. Here there was a central arched light with narrower square-headed lights on either side. In the Gothic revival, rounded or arched windows were reintroduced, but now both upper and lower sections slid vertically. Another Gothic style was to place two light, square-headed windows side by side topped by a common moulding on the wall.

Often glazing bars were completely eliminated, particularly in the mid-19th century as larger sheets of plate glass became available. Unfortunately you should not assume that plate glass is necessarily contemporary with the window frames. Often in the later 19th century the glazing bars of an 18th century sash were knocked out and the small panes they formed replaced by single plate glass panes as owners sought to modernise.

Window Heads and Surrounds

The outside mouldings above windows added much to the pleasing appearance of houses. Originally, in the Middle Ages such 'hood' or 'weather' moulds were purely functional: to protect the window opening from rain-water running down the wall surface. Soon, however, they were also regarded as decorative features, arched or square-head mouldings complementing the overall house design.

Windows in stone houses were given arches to support the walling above the window and these took various forms, with segmental arches and flat arches replacing the medieval round and pointed Gothic ones. In brick houses similarly segmental, cambered and flat arches were the norm, often in a contrasting brick for the arch and the surrounds. These were used to enhance design while the key stones or central bricks of the arches projected and were often carved. While this was common from the 17th to the early 19th centuries, it became less widespread as the trend was to plainer facades.

Moulded classical window surrounds, known as architraves, were popular in larger houses of the 18th century. They spread to smaller houses, villas and

127

even artisan terraces in the later 19th century, partly with the popularity of Italianate styles in the Victorian era, often with small pediments and cornices over the window heads.

The Side-Hung Casement Window

In rural areas and particularly in the north of England, the tradition of mullioned windows never died away entirely and in some cases timber sashes were fitted between the mullions, replacing the iron frames and leaded lights. But while the vertical sash ousted all rivals from the better houses, in the house built in stone and for the smaller country cottage, the side-hung casement or the horizontally-sliding sash were still preferred. These were used to replace the older mullioned windows in many a smaller house and cottage and were not only cheaper to construct but better suited to the squatter window openings in such houses. In the country too, cast-iron casements divided into small panes were a popular replacement for the timber frame, usually but not always in the cottages built for estate workers, such as those at Blyth in Nottinghamshire built for the Mellishes in the 1770s. The village blacksmith added their construction to his skills.

Another development was the 'Yorkshire' sash, very popular in that part of the country but spreading elsewhere too and in the south known as the 'Norfolk' sash. Here, a half of the window slid open horizontally, running in grooves top and bottom. But again the smaller dwellings, if they were glazed at all, generally had fixed windows with perhaps just one small pane that opened.

By the middle of the 19th century, with the Industrial Revolution in full swing, both iron and bigger sheets of glass were being produced in great quantity. Architects used them to glaze large areas, both in public buildings, like the 1851 Crystal Palace or the termini for the new railways, and in conservatories, so fashionable for the Victorian family house. Factory made wrought-iron window frames were appearing too, often with elaborate designs of curve and tracery.

Today factory made windows are available in a variety of materials and styles: sash and casement, 'Georgian' and even leaded lights. Depressingly, the manufacturers' designers appear to have little grounding in the proportions and detailing of the historical styles they ape and most modern windows are unsuitable as straight replacements for historic ones, however simple the design. Indeed, restoration work and replacement of old windows can be a tricky business and skilled joiners are needed to replicate old windows that are beyond repair.

Dormer Windows

The introduction of the chimney stack and the 'chambering over' of hall houses

128

With the introduction of chimney stacks, the roof space could be floored over, thus creating an upper storey which could be used for accommodation with the addition of a dormer window set into the roof. From the 18th century the dormer window commonly lit the upper storey of cottages with their upper rooms partly in the roof.

heralded the beginning of everyday two-storey living. But there were problems in lighting and ventilating the newly-created first floor rooms. There was generally little space for a window, since the walls were fairly low and only a few feet of them rose into the upper floor. Building technology was not advanced enough to provide waterproof skylights in the sloping sides of the roof, so the solution was the dormer window, set vertically under its own miniature roof, pitched at right angles to the main one. The upper rooms, with their inclined ceilings, could really only be used for sleeping and the word dormer derives from the Latin *dormitorium* or sleeping room.

The commonest form of dormer roof is a pitched inverted V, but another technique was to raise the ends of some of the rafters in the main roof and rest them over the top of the window. In thatch areas, the roof covering was then swept over the irregular frame of rafters, producing a pleasing curved effect and what is known as an 'eyebrow' window. When tiles were used to roof the section over the raised rafters above the dormer window the term is 'swept dormer'.

With the pitched dormer roof there are waterproofing problems in the angles where it meets the main roof. With thatch this could be overcome without much difficulty by weaving together the reed or straw to provide a continuous covering, and with stone tiles the courses could be laid to sweep neatly over the junction. In plain tiled roofs, the 'valley' was filled with specially shaped tiles, but for slates and pantiles, strips of lead were required at the junctions.

The style of the dormer roof echoed that of the main one – being hipped if the roof was hipped, gabled if it was gabled – but the position of the dormer varied considerably. In traditional practice dormers were only used where there

129

was no gable which could be used to light the end rooms of a house. Often on cottages there will only be a central dormer to light a central room. The precise location of a dormer in the roof depended on whether there was any vertical wall between the floor and the roof slope. In what are known as 'one and a half storey' or 'one storey and an attic' cottages the dormer window sits on the roof eaves above two or three feet of upper storey wall. In larger buildings, usually where there are two full storeys below the roof, the dormer sits in the middle third of the roof slope.

The modern practice of providing rows of dormers with their eaves almost touching has no basis in traditional practice and should be avoided, as should the practice of using a large 'box dormer' to create additional headroom or even a complete room in the roof. The sole function of a dormer in a historic house is to provide light and ventilation. It is also true that dormers do not look good in shallow pitched roofs and they are almost always associated with thatched or tiled roofs, rather than slate.

There are distinct regional variations. The characteristic Cotswold dormer, for instance, has a steeply-pointed gable and a straight continuation of the front wall above the eaves to the window sill. In areas where Dutch gables were popular, the dormer surround would follow this style in a reduced form, and dormers in Georgian houses reflected the classical embellishments seen around the doors and windows.

While the building of dormer windows began in the Middle Ages and they continued to be widely used in the 16th and 17th centuries, it was in the 18th that they really came into their own, especially in the countryside where agriculture was thriving. Farms were growing in size and in production and more labour was needed. The workers slept in the attic rooms, lit by dormer windows added to old houses to light the new plastered out lofts, or in houses provided with dormers from the start. In the towns too, where building room was increasingly scarce, dormers in the roof enabled more space to be used.

Just as today loft extensions provide extra rooms, so too house owners through the centuries have extended their living space, and many a dormer is actually an addition to a house rather than part of the original building. It is sometimes difficult to tell this in houses built before the 18th century. After this period as dormers became widespread, it is more than likely that they are original.

Doors

An ancient way to describe an intended visit to someone was to say that you were going to 'darken his door', a phrase that is still used in angry dismissal: 'Never darken my door again!' It was accurate symbolism, for in our earliest houses the doorway was not only the way of going in and out, but also the sole source of light for the gloomy windowless interiors. It would be left open during the day and the door only shut at night. At really low social levels there might not even be a door and the opening would be blocked temporarily at night, perhaps by an animal hide, by a lattice of wattle, or even by building up stone slabs.

EARLY DOORS

The standard solution was to butt together a series of vertical planks and secure them with two or three internal horizontal cross-members or ledges. The odd diagonal plank or two might be added for further stability or, in another variation, an extra-stout, double-thickness door could be made with an outer layer of vertical planks and an inner layer of horizontal ones (battens), the two secured to each other with wooden pegs or stout hand-made iron nails. These doors were always of different wood, usually oak on the outer or weather side and elm on the inner. The different warping and shrinking characteristics of oak and elm cancelled each other out to produce a straight door.

Many of these medieval double layered doors can still be seen in parish churches and a few survive in manor houses. Some doors had added character given by wooden fillets covering the vertical joints, but most have long since vanished. Throughout the centuries, however, the basic technique continued to be used for more menial doors, and today you will find the doors of garages, garden sheds and cottages constructed in this way, usually called 'ledged-and-braced' doors.

The early doors were heavy affairs, generally made of hardwood, usually oak. Since it would clearly have been troublesome to heave them daily in and out of position, they hinged at the side. The earliest device was a simple strap of metal around the door, slotting over a vertical pin in the wall opening. Since at first there was no door frame as such, the pin was fixed straight into the wall –

The doorway of the Jew's House in Lincoln is a rare example of a Norman town house. Note the enriched semi-circular arch and the carved capitals on each side below it.

either into the stone surround or into one of the vertical studs of a timber framed house.

In shape, the top of the doorway showed many variations. It might be square-headed or in an arched curve, reflecting the style of the period and reiterating the detail of the window surrounds. In the 14th and 15th centuries, the two-centred arch was popular, but by the late 15th, the four-centred arch had appeared, a shape that continued to be used well into the 17th century, gradually becoming flatter. Other variations include the ogee and the shouldered arch. Mouldings above the door to deflect rainwater repeated those above the windows, except at their ends where mason or carpenter would add decorated stops or corbels. Later in the medieval period drip courses all along the wall were introduced following the line of the windows and another variant is a horizontal drip mould with 'dropped and returned ends'.

There were intriguing regional differences in the size of the doors in medieval houses. They were all generally a little lower than modern doors, which let less heat escape when they were open. By and large they were more or less the same width as we would expect today: between 2 ft 10 inches and 3 ft. But in some parts of England, notably in the West Country, the doors were often much wider. This was a hangover of the longhouse tradition where the doorway had to be wide enough to allow cattle to enter the building, for as we saw earlier, in the true longhouse the owner and his cattle lived under the same roof, albeit at different ends. Farmers are conservative folk and when the longhouse was but a distant memory with the animals long banished, their entrance doorways retained their traditional widths.

Another characteristic of the West, and of Wales too, was the early introduction of a proper door frame, something that was not to become widespread until the 16th century. Having the door hinged on strap and pin meant that it did not fit perfectly and the wind whistled coldly through the cracks. Rebating the frame, whether in stone or timber, gave the door something to close against and reduced draughts. To obtain an even better fit, doors needed a neater hanging arrangement. The answer was the hinge – and its design and manufacture became another skill of the local blacksmith. Hinges came in all sorts of shapes and sizes, from simple L- and H-shaped ones to intricate and highly-decorated designs. The weight of the door, however, meant that they had to be much sturdier than those of today, which gives them a certain charm and makes them well worth retaining as a feature in older houses.

Early doors had other pieces of monumental ironmongery attached to them. There might be a wrought-iron grille set in, an early 'spy-hole' to monitor callers, and the door would be secured at night with a heavy draw-bar slotted into brackets on the wall or door frame. This was later replaced or augmented

133

By the 15th century plank and ledge doors fixed with iron hinges onto a snugly fitting door frame made houses more secure and comfortable.

The early 17th century saw the introduction of the panelled door, giving scope for more variety in design and decoration.

with a stout lock. These again were at first much bigger and clumsier than modern designs, and were fitted with the large keys that have now become popular collectors' items.

▨ PANELLED DOORS ▨

The heavy doorways of medieval, Tudor and Elizabethan times became old fashioned, as well as being heavy to hang and open. New ideas arrived from France and the Netherlands and were eagerly adopted for doors and walls, although panelling and panelled doors were well known in medieval times, many surviving in chancel screens. Linen fold panelling of the Tudor years had been adapted for internal doors, but the Continental influence led to the introduction of the panelled exterior door. Apart from using less wood, the framing preserved the strength of the older varieties.

The panelled door consists of an open frame strengthened with a few horizontal and vertical cross-members tenoned in, with the gaps between filled with thinner wooden panels, either set in rebates or in slots cut in the frame timbers. It requires greater carpentry skills, of course, but the result is more aesthetically pleasing and gives added scope for variety in design and decoration. In the 17th century very elaborate doors were designed, some with lozenges formed by the framing and others with built up panels, or the frame members would be decorated with patterns of nails or the panels themselves would be carved in low relief or incised with foliage of a vaguely classical nature. Increasingly as the century wore on the more correct six and eight panel door became the norm in town houses. By the early 18th century the six-panelled door was commonplace, the upper pair being relatively small and the middle pair the largest: all carefully proportioned in accordance with classical principles. Later doors were made with more panels of differing sizes and shapes, such as the eight-panelled one, arranged in rows of – starting at the top – two, three, one and two panels.

The panels themselves could be flat or raised ('fielded' is the technical term) and they slotted into grooves in the door frame and cross-members. The look of the door was further enhanced by shaping the timbers and by the addition of decorative mouldings, either applied or cut into the framing members, which in the former case also concealed any gap between panel and door member. The panels were intentionally cut to be a loose fit so they could absorb any shrinkage or warping in the door frame without splitting.

The introduction of the panelled door meant that lighter hinges could be used and it also led to the introduction of butt hinges, which are concealed between the door and its outer frame. They are the standard fixtures for modern doors.

TUDOR, ELIZABETHAN AND GEORGIAN DOORS

By late Tudor and early Elizabethan times the doorway was well on the way to becoming one of the principal architectural features of a house, particularly for larger properties. Often it was set in an outer lobby or porch that carried on upwards to the full height of the building with rooms over. The woodwork or stone was intricately carved, and during the Elizabethan period the porch and doorways were being framed by pediments, pilasters and columns.

In some parts of the country, notably in the stone-building area around the Lake District and the Pennines, examples can be found of doorways which are really a curious hybrid of earlier styles with glimmerings of the Renaissance and Palladianism. Stone lintels are common and it was popular to carve their undersides to represent a four centred arch or a stylised classical cornice. Later the lintels would be more intricately carved, and decorated with dates, initials and heraldic devices. Mouldings above the doorway would mimic battlements or arches and, later still, the whole upper doorway would begin to take on the Georgian look, often in a half-understood form.

The classical Georgian door, easily identified by its columns and elaborate pediments.

In the classical revival the doorway reached its zenith as an architectural feature, and even doors in smaller houses reflected the influence of the new ideas in art and architecture. Canopies and pediments were the order of the day by the late 17th and early 18th centuries, often supported on richly carved brackets, some in the shape of cherubs or Atlas figures holding up their burden of the door hood. Square-headed door surrounds were commonest, particularly early on, but the style developed into a variety of shapes, sizes and decorations. There were triangular pediments and curved ones, pediments shaped like

136

scrolls, pediments broken and enhanced with a central decoration. The semi-circular arch was popular too, with a large keystone often initialled and dated, and also the square-headed doorway surmounted by a lintel to imitate stepped voussoirs (the wedge-shaped blocks of an arch).

In all but the humblest houses the front door opened into a hall, or at least a porch, and this was lit by a fanlight above the door, usually semi-circular in shape. Nowhere in England can this flowering of the door's development be better seen than in the houses put up in London's building boom in the 18th century, not only in elaborate pediments and cornices and delicate low reliefs, but also in the classical columns that now commonly surrounded the door – some squared, some rounded, others reflecting the full vigour of the Doric and Ionic orders. Over the sea, Dublin is rightly famed for its vast and wonderfully rich collection of Georgian doorways in its 18th century town houses and terraces.

The doors themselves were more often than not of six panels and generally made in pine or deal, which was painted. Unfortunately there is now a fad for stripping the protective paint off these doors: the architect would turn in his grave. Inside richer houses hardwood was still used, usually veneered with mahogany, occasionally walnut or maple, just like the best contemporary furniture.

The classical doorway eventually fell from fashion, not least because of a succession of Building Acts in London, which discouraged the use of projecting timber work on facades. As a consequence in London and areas influenced by London, stone and stuccoed brick columns and pediments replaced the timber door surrounds. The porch receded from favour too, although in the later 18th century its place was often taken by a trellis-like open structure of ornamental cast iron – a fashionable addition both to newly-built houses and to older properties. The porch, now usually stuccoed and columned, underwent a major revival in the 19th century, as seen in miles of terraces in Bayswater, Belgravia, Pimlico, Brighton or Cheltenham.

▨ VICTORIAN AND MODERN DOORS ▨

In Georgian times glass had been used in front doors, usually in place of the two small upper panels. Bulls-eyes or bullions were used, that is the central knob discarded from circular sheets of crown glass. These were in effect waste material and normally only used by those who could not afford clear glass from the rest of the sheet. However, in fashionable houses these bullions were used to light the hall while at the same time preserving privacy: an early form of obscured glazing.

With the rapid development of glass-making techniques of the 19th century,

137

Glass in doors made its appearance in early Victorian times and by the mid-19th century it was often coloured in geometric patterns of panes.

sheets of glass began to make their appearance in doors, at first replacing the wood in the upper two panels. The availability of these larger sheets of glass speeded the adoption of the four panel door, with the two upper panels often now occupying over half the height of the door. The mid-19th century availability of plate glass led to the two panel door in which a single large sheet of glass took up most of the upper half of the door. So that it still let in light but prevented the glances of the curious, the glass would be etched with acid, or have stained or coloured glass, often as geometric patterns set in leaded lights. Such doors tended to be out of fashion in the 20th century and were replaced, but if they do still remain in a Victorian house, they should be retained, renovated and repainted. It might prove a little difficult to find the glass, but there are still specialised firms which should be able to help.

Domestic architecture in the 20th century has seen such a bewildering variety of styles and revivals that it is impossible to generalise about developments with doors. Medieval-style plank doors, with metal studs, showed up again in many a suburban development, as did doors with leaded lights, perhaps with coloured sun-bursts or curious Art Deco designs, popular in the 1930s. Also making its mark in the 1920s (although there are earlier examples) was the glazed or French door, almost totally of glass and usually with 15 panes, arranged in five rows of three. While it was occasionally used as a front door, it found most favour in the double version – a pair of French windows leading out into the garden. In the 1960s and 1970s the Georgian door made a comeback, even in small houses with no other pretensions to classical symmetry, the door itself usually a wholly inaccurate interpretation of Georgian models. Today, however, householders seem able to choose a new front door from most periods of history in many different veneers of wood, however inappropriate or poorly designed.

▧ DOOR FURNITURE ▧

Early doors, as we have seen, would be 'furnished' on the inside with a drawbar and perhaps also a large lock, while on the outside the straps of the hinges could be seen, with also a key hole and possibly a pattern of metal studs. Locks later evolved so that they could be fitted within the thickness of the door itself, something that is commonplace today. But two other items of door furniture are comparatively recent additions: the door knocker and the letter box. Knobs, knockers and handles evolved in the 18th century, and although the very best were in brass they were usually made in cast iron, and painted. So if you want your house to look authentic, there is really no need to go to all the bother and expense of brass, although it seems that few people can resist it. Whatever 'furniture' you fit, though, take care that it suits the shape and symmetry of the door.

Letter boxes arrived with the Penny Post after 1840, as before the age of the pre-paid postage stamp the postman or letter carrier had to knock to obtain payment from the recipient. You can still see the elegant very early letter boxes, usually in cast-iron. They are smaller than today's with slots no wider than four inches by an inch high, the flap often with the word 'Letters' cast in.

139

Floors and Ceilings

For hundreds of years – even up to the 18th century in the lowliest houses – the ground floor of the house was simply beaten earth. While neither clean nor hygienic by modern standards, a well-laid floor can provide a surprisingly solid surface, not all that dissimilar to concrete. The secret lay in the preparation of the ground and in the mixing-in of certain natural additives with the earth, to meld it together. The basic technique was to dig over the ground and rake the earth painstakingly to produce a tilth as fine as that in a seed bed. Then gallon upon gallon of water would be poured over it and the resulting quagmire allowed to drain, settle and dry out, a process that might take as long as a month, but which resulted in a hard compacted skin to the floor, with a texture rather like baked mud. This would be uneven, so the final task was *melling*, beating the floor flat with wooden paddles.

Among the additives mixed with the earth to make it even more solid and durable were lime (which was used from earlier medieval times in districts where it was readily available), sand, bone chips and fine clay. Bulls' blood was sometimes used too, to give a dense dark surface which could even be polished.

Despite the maker's best endeavours, though, beaten earth floors were dusty and in an effort to keep this down, especially in summer, they were strewn with straw, rushes or grasses. If this covering was changed regularly when it dried out or began to smell too much, then the floors could be kept clean and tidy. But the 16th century English, it seems, were far from fastidious in this, judging by a letter written by Erasmus, who stayed in Britain in the early 1500s. He told a friend: 'The floors are commonly of clay, strewed with rushes, under which lies unmolested an ancient collection of beer, grease, fragments, bones, spittle, excrement of dogs and cats and everything that is nasty.'

There was obviously some nastiness seeping into the floors, not only from cat and dog excrement but from human urine as well, for our ancestors were not too bothered about sanitation. Whatever its source, the result was that the floors soaked up material rich in nitre – the 'saltpetre' used in making gunpowder. Since this was scarce, the Crown turned to floors as a rich source of much-needed war material, and empowered 'saltpetre men' to enter people's homes, dig up and take away their floors. The Crown was supposed to make good any damage but, as this was seldom done, the visits of the saltpetre men were far from welcome, especially as they also had powers to remove earth walls – those of cob, for instance – if necessary. It was not until the Commonwealth period that the saltpetre men's powers of 'common seisin' were revoked.

Gradually, and as usual starting with better-class homes, earthen floors were replaced with more solid covering. Stone slabs had long been used in those areas where suitable rock was in good supply but their use spread down the social scale. Also small stones or 'pitchings' were laid when slabs were not available or too costly and these could be collected from the fields. Elsewhere alternatives had to be found, such as brick and clay tiles, which were in common use for floors by the 17th century. Early floor tiles were larger than those of today and were unglazed. Glazed tiles were an 18th century development, which saw full flowering in the magnificent mosaic tiles used in striking patterns in Georgian and Victorian entrance halls.

In the 18th century, timber floors were brought in for living rooms, stone and tiles being retained only in kitchens and other service rooms, such as the laundry.

▨ UPPER FLOORS ▨

Owing to the fact that the top section of medieval houses was filled with smoke from the fire burning in the central hearth (see Fireplaces p 154), whole upper floors were uncommon before the 14th century, although wings with upstairs rooms were usually found at one or both ends of the open hall. These were floored in wooden boards resting on flat joists, which could be decoratively carved or moulded. The boards were often laid loose and not seen as part of the house: in Tudor and earlier wills the floorboards are recorded as bequeathed just like other possessions such as beds. Even when floorboards became permanently fixed to their joists it was not normal to plaster the underside of floors, so boards and joists were visible as the ceiling of the room below.

The development of proper chimneys from the 15th century onwards removed the smoke from the upper part of the hall and meant that extra accommodation could be provided by a complete 'flooring over' or 'chambering over'. By careful investigation it is possible to tell if a floor was a later addition to the house, or whether it was put in during the original building. If the roof is original then there will be traces of sooty deposits on its beams and rafters, from the fires that would have burned almost continuously in the open hearth below.

In Wealden houses (see p 16), found principally in the south of England, the central section would certainly have been a full height hall open to the roof, so an inserted floor in the middle must be a later addition. For other types it is

141

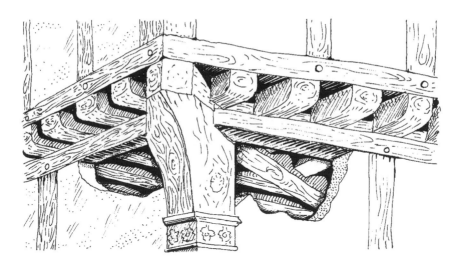

In timber buildings with an upper storey, jettying on two adjacent sides was made possible by using dragon beams, protruding from the house corner into which the floor joists would be jointed.

sometimes more difficult to find out, although for the discerning eye there are differences in the quality of the timber between the floor joists and supporting beams, and those of the wall beams and studs. And study the joints between the main beam of the ceiling and wall timbers. If the beam has been added later the carpenters would have had problems in squeezing it into position, so the joint will generally be less snug than if the beam was put in when the house was built, or it may merely rest on one of the older horizontal beams.

There are those purists who, on discovering the first floor is a later addition, have removed it to restore the hall to its medieval proportions. This is fine if you do not need the accommodation, but hardly necessary; the first floor was a welcome innovation, adding convenience and comfort to the house.

One of the interesting techniques of medieval carpenters, who possessed considerable woodworking skills, was that they appeared to lay their floor joists the wrong way round; that is wider across than deep. This has puzzled many who think they got it wrong: in fact the medieval carpenter knew his oak perfectly. The house was carpentered in 'green' oak which is easier to work than hard dry seasoned timber. Warping was a consequent problem, so in order to keep the warping in the right plane the medieval carpenter made his joists wider than they were deep, the greater depth absorbing the warping as the oak dried out within the plane of the floor. The other way round would have produced a wavy floor. When timber was plentiful joists could be massive, as much

142

as 8 inches wide by 5 inches deep, but later the carpenters reduced the joists to square dimensions: still perfectly adequate but more liable to warp in all directions. Oak is of course a flexible timber, so many structural engineers are nervous of its qualities, and one can find quite springy floors but this is not necessarily anything to be worried about unless the joists are rotten.

It was not until the 17th century, it seems, when the more brittle softwoods were increasingly used that carpenters adapted their technique and turned their joists on edge. Nowadays of course all timbers have to be thus for virtually all building is in these softwoods that cannot 'flex' or bend, so the depth of a softwood joist is more than its medieval counterpart, although much narrower.

Timber-framed houses were (and are) creaky places and where joists met wall timbers the joints would creak, so when the upper floor was being used the medieval house was a noisy place. The problem was partly overcome, no doubt unintentionally, by the fashion for 'jettying' the upper storeys, a technique imported from the Continent in the 14th century and widely used from the 15th to the 17th centuries; and discussed in the chapter on Walls (p 104). The extension of the floor joists over the ground floor walls may have reduced the tendency for floor joists to sag, but as we have seen their main purpose was a non-structural one: to demonstrate the owner was prosperous enough to have at least part of his house built on two (or more) floors. Certainly jettying was immensely popular and the challenge to the carpenter was to provide jetties on more than one side. Here he used the 'dragon beam', a substantial diagonal joist protruding from the house corner into which the joists of each side were tenoned. In a normal floor the joists only went one way but as jettying was formed by projecting the joists it necessitated joists laid in more than one direction in a single room. The dragon beam formed the junction between these joists which met at right angles. They were called dragon beams because their exposed ends, or the post that supports them at the corner of the house, were often carved with dragons.

The first floor could be further strengthened, and its span increased, by the use of a massive central ceiling beam, into which the joists were tenoned. Such beams are called summers or summer trees, the word deriving from the Anglo-Norman *somer*, itself a derivative of the Latin and Greek words for pack-horse. And that is apt, for the summer takes the load of the ceiling and the upper floor on its back. It commonly ran from wall to chimney breast and – though the accompanying joists may have been plastered over – usually the summer was left exposed, its lines frequently softened by chamfering and carved and moulded designs. It is now more commonly called a 'spine beam'. The shape and style of such details can give useful clues to dating the house. Contrary to the general rule, the decoration of summer, joist and 'stop moulds' at the joints seems to get less elaborate as time goes on.

143

Where the joists are also chamfered and stopped this means that the ceiling was not plastered and often indicates the best room when the house was built, for other rooms may have plain joists. This is not an infallible guide, needless to say, for during the 17th century and certainly by 1700 plastered ceilings became the norm and huge numbers of open joists were covered and only the spine-beam remained exposed.

Floorboards were originally planks of oak or elm, although when good wood became scarcer and increased in price, cheaper alternatives such as pine and deal were used. Also, as a general rule, floorboards have become narrower over the centuries, early examples being a foot or more in width. Until well into the 19th century the boards were merely butted together: tongue-and-groove boarding is a comparatively recent innovation.

Wood was not the only material used for upper floors, although it was the commonest. Plaster, earth, even stone were used too. Despite the large size of the timber joists required to support the weight of stone upper floors, these were built as late as the Georgian period.

Floors of plaster were especially prevalent in the East Midlands, not only in smaller houses but in quite superior ones as well. The use of plaster was due in part to timber shortages, but some builders suggested it gave a better, more even finish which would not warp or settle. The floor joists, and supporting beams where necessary, were laid in the same way as for floorboards, but then a bed of straw or reeds was laid across them over which was trowelled a covering of plaster, as much as 2 inches thick. The best ingredient for the plaster was gypsum, although lime was also used, particularly in the Cotswolds. Clay or burnt brick were added as the aggregate. Plaster, however, while being strong in compression is weaker in tension, and plaster floors had a tendency to crack when heavy loads, like the bed or old oak chest, were put on them. Earth or mud upper floors were occasionally made in areas where gypsum or lime were hard to come by, but they tended to be relegated to less important areas like lofts.

▨ CEILINGS ▨

A favourite expression of estate agents selling old houses is 'with a wealth of exposed timbers'. Very fine such houses look, but it is important to remember that, as with the timber in walls, not all ceiling beams and joists were meant to be exposed. In the better quality medieval houses, joist and summer, and the underside of the floorboards, were left uncovered, but where the joists were of rough-hewn timber there would have been some covering-up. This was done by packing the space between the joists with a filling of clay and straw, which was then plastered over.

By the 16th century owners of better quality houses led the fashion for covering the ceiling beams and joists behind a false ceiling. It was then plastered and ornamented like this Elizabethan example.

By the 16th century the owners of better-quality homes were demanding plastered ceilings, both for the sake of appearance and for insulation, and by the 18th century this was the rule rather than the exception in all but the smallest houses and cottages. Also, the process of modernisation of old properties continued and even those ceilings with fine decorated oak beams and joists which were intended to be on show were covered over with a layer of plaster. There are even cases where a whole false ceiling, with its own supporting joists, was suspended beneath the first floor, so the deep summers could be hidden beneath a smooth surface. The basis for the plaster was a series of timber laths nailed to the underside of the joists. At first these were 'riven', oak split by hand, but by the 19th century sawn softwood laths came into use, so examining these can give another clue to dating.

Early builders also often put insulation between the ceiling and the first floor, using chaff and straw between the joists, which not only increased the fire risk but provided a cosy haven for rats and mice.

The substances used in the plaster varied from area to area, but a popular recipe was a mix of lime and sand with cowhair added for binding strength.

145

Ornamental plasterwork on cornices and covering was very much the vogue in mid-Victorian homes.

Gypsum, which is widely used today, was at first confined to areas where it occurred naturally, in the East Midlands, for instance. Decorators were unable to resist the extra opportunities that plaster gave them to show off their skills and from the late 16th century particularly there are many fine examples of decorative work and intricate mouldings, especially in friezes.

When restoring old property it is common practice to expose the timber beams, and this invariably produces a pleasing effect, even if they were not originally intended to be seen. One of the hazards of this task is the evil black dust that emanates if that old-fashioned insulation was used; but one of the joys is discovering chamfered and decorated summers and joists that may have been hidden for generations.

Staircases

The staircase started life as a purely functional piece of household equipment, a rude and crude means of ascending and descending to and from the upper floors. It gradually became less cramped and inconvenient and it evolved through the magnificent joinery work of Elizabethan, Jacobean and Commonwealth staircases, and the soaring, curving splendour of Georgian stairs, to be the finest and most prominent interior architectural feature of the house. But then its importance declined again, function rather than form and style seeming the major requirement in modern times.

As with most social changes, the grander houses set the fashion whether for staircases, or fireplaces, doors and windows – and provided the inspiration for change and development on a smaller scale in lesser houses.

In the earliest houses, of course, there was no need for a staircase, most homes being single-storey affairs. At higher levels of society, though, staircases were needed and examples include the stone houses of the late 12th and 13th century, popularly known as King John Houses, where the living rooms were on the upper floor, generally reached by a straight flight of stone steps on the outside. In upper-floor hall houses access was again by external steps. These outside staircases were often roofed: the best surviving example is not on a house but the superb Norman one at Canterbury Cathedral Priory. There are, of course, large numbers of stone spiral or newel staircases surviving in churches and castles, often set within the thickness of the walls or attached to the outside in a semi-circular turret, such as the Anglo-Saxon one at Brixworth church in Northamptonshire. Newel stairs survive in tower houses in the north of England, with storage room at the base, living accommodation on the first floor, and bedrooms on second and, possibly, subsequent storeys. These storeys were similarly connected by a spiral staircase, either built into the thickness of the walls or accommodated in its own small projecting turret.

The owner of the everyday early medieval house lived, slept and ate at ground level, with nothing between his floor and the smoky roof above his head. As time progressed, part of the hall or extra bays would be divided off into more private rooms, and upper rooms formed above their flat ceilings. These would usually be reached by a straight ladder resting against the partition wall, or later by a more elaborate but no less cramped and inconvenient companion-

In medieval times the domestic circular stone staircase was very much a smaller reflection of those built for castles of the age.

way. Quite a few early medieval stairways survive and these consisted of two straight timbers set about 18 inches apart with triangular section baulks of oak pegged to them, thus the treads were solid and heavy. A much improved and considerably lighter carpentered version was more usual in merchant and manor houses and became the norm – a series of treads resting on 'strings', that is the side timbers supporting the stairs, cut to carry them. Others had the stair ends mortised into straight strings (the timber side planks holding the treads).

The stairs, in whatever form, passed through the ceiling by cutting short one or more joists and 'trimming' them by mortise and tenons into a short cross beam. A popular style of stair among carpenters, and one that lasted into the

An early 17th century framed newel staircase with straight flights and square landings.
This style enabled the carpenter to show off his skills with carefully carved posts topped
with elaborate finials.

20th century, enclosed the stairs in a shallow cupboard to carry the treads and
strings and to support the ends of the two or three floor joists cut back to take
the stairway. It reduced heat loss and was structurally simple but is now seldom
to be seen except in cottages, having been replaced by more sophisticated versions. Although it does survive in the primitive 'cogloft' cottages of Wales and
Ireland and, in more substantial form, in the straight-flight stone steps that were
built into some of the better medieval houses.

As the hall house developed, with the addition of either one or two double-storeyed wings or with a complete upper floor covering the whole of the house area, more staircases were obviously needed, but narrow straight flights or cramped spirals were all that were on offer for centuries.

The spiral staircase was the everyday reflection of the stone spirals of medieval castles. Tight and steeply-stepped, it turned in a complete half circle and for this reason the stairways were often known as caracoles, from the French term *caracoler*, for a horse and rider to execute a turn to left or right. The steps would be made of stone, or from solid wooden planks slotted into the timber walls and radiating from a central mast-like pole or newel. The stairs might be built around the fireplace, the space between the chimney stack and wall being very convenient, or they might be tucked into some other internal corner. Alternatively, and particularly in stone-building areas, the stairway was contained in a semi-circular bulge projecting from the building, often in the angle where hall and two-storeyed wing met.

Staircases gradually became less cramped, a significant breakthrough in their development coming in the 16th century when the fireplace moved. From being built on the line of an outside wall, the chimney was moved to the middle of the house, and the staircase could conveniently curve around its massive stack. This innovation seems first to have occurred in the south-eastern counties of England in Elizabeth I's reign and is particularly associated with the 'lobby entry' plan where the entrance lobby was formed in front of the stack and the staircase behind it. And although it soon spread elsewhere in the country, it was by no means universal. In the Midlands, in Cambridgeshire and Huntingdonshire, for instance, the stack usually stood free and unencumbered by stairs.

By the end of the 16th century many of the larger houses had become three-storeyed, with not only a first floor but another above it, creating rooms in the roof space. Tight spirals or cramped straight flights were therefore even more inconvenient. One solution was to ascend each floor in three flights, with right-angled turns between them, so the stairs still described a 180 degree turn. The steps were made of stone or timber, arranged around a solid central core of stone or brick. Such staircases were easier to use than the tight spiral, but took up about three times the space of a winding stair. So in smaller houses a common arrangement was to have two instead of three flights, the second reversing the direction of the first at a half-landing. This configuration was known as a 'dog-leg' stair or 'a pair of stairs'.

To give more room for the larger staircase, a special wing or outshut was often built on the wall of the house. This was a common feature in the south and east in the early 17th century and became widespread in the Midlands between 1650 and 1700. Another way of gaining more space was to build a storeyed porch at the front of the house, containing both entrance door and staircase, a style that was popular in the Lake District and a few other parts of the north.

The three-flight arrangement around a solid core gave little scope for display and decoration, so it soon developed into a grander staircase which gave more chance to the carpenter to show off his skills and the owner to impress his neighbours. This was the framed newel staircase, in which the central core is abolished and replaced by newel posts at the angles of each of the turns, creating an open well. Elaborate carving on the newels and balusters turned the staircases into works of art and, in a later development, into works of great joinery skill too. Here the newels were shortened to become separate posts at each landing, again carefully carved and often topped with beautifully designed finials. By this time the stairs themselves were formed of two planks, a 'riser' and a 'tread' which helped reduce weight and allowed for more elaborate and complex carpentry.

Balusters, the curving pillars supporting the rail were a product of the Renaissance revival, emanating from its northern French and Netherlandish versions. The name itself derives from the Greek *balaustion*, the wild pomegranate flower, whose shape they were supposed to resemble. Early versions, however, were tubby imitations of the classical design and in cheaper versions were often not turned but profiled from planks of oak, and known as 'splat' balusters. Magnificent wooden staircases reached their zenith in Jacobean and Commonwealth times, with a variety of intricate designs and elaborate woodwork. By the end of the 17th century owners wanted to have a framed staircase rising impressively from the central hall. The fashion for the central fireplace and chimney stack, however, meant that there was not enough space for an imposing staircase – and so the chimney changed its position, back to the gable ends, to make way for the staircase.

As the 18th century progressed stairways became ever lighter and more graceful, with slimmer balusters in greater number. The Georgian house plan eliminated for ever the great chimney in the centre of the house. In the medium-size and larger dwellings the entrance door was centred on the house front and opened into a large hall filled with what had now become the most prominent interior architectural feature: the staircase. Later in this period the development of iron-smelting with coke meant the increasing use of ironwork in architecture and even more beautiful staircase designs with elegant and intricate cast-iron or wrought-iron balustrades and delicate sweeping curves. As the staircase was often central and away from the windows, it needed its own source of light and another Georgian feature is the small lantern or turret capped with a glass cupola, lighting the staircase from above. More light also came from the glass fan above the door.

The Georgian house plan had no need of a great chimney in the centre of the house, so opening up the entrance hall for a large and imposing staircase. As the 18th century progressed staircases became lighter and more graceful with slimmer balusters, some even made of delicate ironwork.

In smaller houses, however, there was no room for such magnificence and because of the lack of space the dog-leg or 'pair of stairs' design more often found favour, particularly in the terraced houses which had begun to make their appearance in the second half of the 18th century. The typical better-class terrace house had a front door opening into a narrowish hall (called a 'passage' in the north) with the dog-leg stairs ascending out of it to a half-landing and then back on themselves to reach the first floor. In many such houses a further boxed-in staircase led to the large attic room. Dog-leg stairs, or even a flight rising from the hall and making just one right-angled turn to the landing, were to become the norm right up to modern times.

152

Even the small Victorian and Edwardian artisan terrace house made something of the staircase and its hall had glazed floor-tiles, often in a simple chequer pattern, with the staircase rising from the narrow hall with a fluted or balustered bottom post or newel. The mahogany or brown painted banister rail descended to curl elegantly round this post and sometimes the bottom stair also has a semi-circular outer edge to the tread, while light might filter into the hallway through stained glass in the fanlight and door.

In the open-plan houses popular in the 1950s and 1960s, open tread staircases (that is with no risers) were often made a feature, but they were generally plain and simple compared with earlier splendours.

Fireplaces and Chimneys

There is no smoke without fire, we say, but the early house-dweller would know only too well that the converse is also true: there is no fire without smoke. A hearth in the home was essential, of course, for winter warmth – and year-round cooking – but while the fire might burn brightly and merrily, medieval houses must have been very draughty or very smoky, or an uncomfortable combination of both. And of course fire was a lethal companion: the Great Fire of London of 1666 was just one of many fires that razed towns, villages and farms. The story of the fireplace and chimney is the story of taming this ravenous flaming beast.

Matters would have been much improved by the Tudor and Elizabethan eras, with great fireplaces and solid chimney stacks taking over from the open hearth; and by Georgian and Regency times, helped by the replacement of wood by coal as a fuel, the fireplace had become not only reasonably efficient but also a focus of ornament and design in stylish rooms. The Victorian fireplace, too, was the dominant feature of the room, if somewhat over-bearing in its shape and structure.

The Romans had brought to Britain sophisticated house-warming systems, including central heating using hot air ducts below the floor, but most homes of ordinary people continued to use the traditional, smoky, sooty method: a large fire for cooking and heating on a central hearth of stones. In Saxon and medieval Britain wood was in plentiful supply and once lit, the fire would be kept burning almost continuously. Slow-burning oak would be the fuel of preference, giving more heat for less smoke. To blaze merrily, though, a fire needs a good supply of air, and that came in through ill-fitting doors, windows and shutters, its cool blasts diverted but hardly halted by strategically placed screens.

The smoke was allowed to escape through a hole in the roof or often through triangular gaps left at the top of the gable ends, but such systems were far from efficient.

An early improvement was to fit the smoke-escape holes with louvres, which while encouraging the smoke outwards kept the rain from coming in. In poorer houses the louvres would be simply made from wattles below a rough thatch, but in better-off homes, especially from the 13th century onwards, timber or pottery louvres, frequently well-decorated, were incorporated, often built into their own chimney-like structures.

The hall house was one of the principal architectural concepts in house-building: a form that existed, with modifications, right up to the 17th century. With the fire burning on its central hearth, use of the upper space in the hall was not practicable, for here the smoke gathered before filtering out through the roof. Later, however, one end of the hall would be partitioned off, or a double-storeyed wing or two would be added on to its central section. Such extra rooms would obviously be cold, being separated from the main hearth, so smaller fire-places were often put in the wall to heat them. The word chimney originally meant fireplace, originating from the Latin *caminata*, a room with a fireplace, which itself derived from the Greek *kaminor*, oven.

Those who lived in tower houses, or upper floor hall houses would have had wall fireplaces as a matter of course, augmented sometimes by a central brazier. The brazier or fire in a fretted bucket on legs, usually three, was much commoner than is generally realised and more and more documentary references to them, particularly in towns, are being found. Mind you, they were even more of a fire hazard than a normal fire, being more liable to be toppled: the portability came with a price. In the grand houses, too, particularly those of a semi fortified nature, wall fireplaces were a common feature.

Wall Fireplaces

The first major improvement in the hall house was to move the principal fireplace from its central hearth to a side wall, a move that usually came in the 15th century. This then allowed the whole of the upper part of the hall to be floored

A major innovation in the medieval hall house was the resiting of the central hearth to a side wall where the smoke was channelled up a large hood. It became common by the 15th century.

155

over, providing two storeys. The smoke from the big wall fireplace was collected in a large, funnel-shaped hood – usually made of timber with thick daub, or in some areas of stone – which might push out up to 5 ft into the room. This hood extended into the second-storey room, where it provided much-needed radiant heat, before ending just below the louvred smoke exits. In some areas platforms were built on either side of the hood, for storage, for seats or even for beds – the cosiest in the house. These forms were popular in the West Country and the north-west.

Alternatively, the chimney stack was built outside the line of the hall, in many ways a better alternative since it helped to keep the hot gases and sparks away from the inflammable thatch. Usually, of course, it was best to put the chimney on the gable end, where it was well clear of the thatch, but in some house designs, such as the hall with two end wings, this was impracticable, so the chimney would be on a side wall (normally the back one). It was easier to build a chimney here since it did not have to extend so high, but it created problems because the joint between the chimney and roof would collect rainwater and be liable to penetrating damp. So the area was often protected by a small pitched roof, set at a right angle to the main roof.

Chimneys were being built in increasing numbers in the 15th century, and most houses had a chimney stack of some kind by the end of the 16th century. But they were not universal, perhaps due to the difficulty in finding skilled craftsmen to build them. A stone chimney required a mason's skills and he would be expensive and difficult to inveigle away from the castle, grand houses and monastery where he found most of his employment, while in most areas bricks were not yet cheap enough for the farmer and peasant. So even in the 16th century, and even in the more advanced south-east of England, some houses still had a central, one-storey hall with a fire burning in an open hearth and its smoke escaping, slowly, out of a hole in the roof. But the Dissolution of the Monasteries released large numbers of masons from their ecclesiastic labours and the expansion in brickmaking helped to usher in the great era of fireplace and chimney building in late Tudor and Elizabethan times.

TUDOR AND ELIZABETHAN FIREPLACES

We have seen how the medieval fireplace extended deep into the room with a wide hearth and a canopy over to take away the smoke. In Tudor times a much more deeply recessed fireplace with a thick external chimney stack became the normal pattern. So much chimney building went on in the 16th century that it became known as 'The Age of Chimneys' and in 1577 an observer wrote of 'the multitude of chimneys lately erected'.

As well as stone, brick was increasingly used for the chimney stack, and the fireplace surround was a fresh ground for the craftsman to carve and decorate. The opening was sometimes properly arched, although more often the lintel was merely carved in an arch shape (usually four centred). At the corners the spandrels could be decorated with some heraldic design.

The Central Stack

The major innovation, however came in around the beginning of the 17th century with the introduction of the central or axial chimney stack which rapidly became popular.

This era also saw the burgeoning of a prosperous middle class, not only of merchants but of affluent farmers looking for better housing than that enjoyed (or endured) by their forefathers. Some might have an axial stack built into their existing houses; others wanted new houses and a mini-industry grew up to meet that demand.

The central chimney was the most expensive feature of the new style houses. It was a really solid structure, built of stone or brick according to the area, and was the first thing to be put up on site. It provided the core of the house, a prop for the whole building. In the case of fire, unfortunately all too common in the 17th century, the chimney might be all that was left standing and would form the basis for rebuilding.

The standardised Elizabethan and Jacobean farmhouse was rectangular in shape, the chimney stack dividing it internally into two rooms, or three with an unheated end room. In plan the chimney stack was in the shape of an H, that is with two fireplaces back to back opening into kitchen and parlour, the latter the successor to the open hall, or less usually into parlour and end room, the successor to the solar. The central stack also provided an ideal place around which to build the staircase.

From the ground floor the wide stack continued upwards, either opening into two more fireplaces in the chambers above in higher status houses or heating them through heat radiating from the stack as it passed though the first floor and attic, and out of the roof. Here in the open air it might be finished off in a cluster of four chimneys while in others beautiful patterns and decorations often made the chimney the house's crowning glory. So much so that it is only a slight exaggeration to suggest that chimney tops were one of England's greatest contributions to the architecture of the Renaissance period.

A point about dating here. Beautiful brick chimneys were a major feature of Tudor building of grand houses (Hampton Court is a classic example), and while those who could afford it quickly aped their betters, fine chimneys in everyday houses are generally of a later period, from the 17th century on.

Axial chimneys were not only built in new houses, but put into existing ones, and their position depended on the size and shape of the house. The fireplace that had become a splendid feature in the great houses and palaces of Tudor and Elizabethan England often reflected that charming half-assimilated Renaissance work that is to be found in other architectural detail of the period, where classical features are intermingled with earlier design and styling. Above the carved over-mantel, for instance, there would often be a series of arched recesses. Another design replaced the over-mantel with a large moulded panel, sometimes ornamented, but often with very clean and simple lines or plaster reliefs, crude copies of grander classical profile medallions: even Red Indians' heads appear in over-mantel reliefs.

▦ The Farm and Cottage Fireplace

Even into the 17th century fireplaces and stacks were formed entirely in timber, heavily daubed over or plastered in an attempt to render them fire-proof. Many of them evolved from the earlier smoke-hood form mentioned earlier, but timber and fire do not make good bed-fellows so relatively few of these survive intact. Many must have burned down and the bulk would have been replaced by brick or stone. Where they do survive they should be carefully safeguarded (probably by not being used!)

In the less imposing homes, and in farmhouses, the fireplace now occupied pride of place, but while it was large in scale it was much simpler in design. The fireplace surround might be dressed in stone or merely have a solid oak beam, called a bressumer, across the top of the opening, shaped to imitate the stone prototype or merely chamfered and supported on pillars of brick or stone. In its simplest form the Elizabethan fireplace showed little or no decoration, the massive lintel being a straight oak beam. In the east and south-east of England, where brick-building techniques were highly developed, the fireplace surround would be framed entirely in moulded bricks. There were often recesses in the sides of the bigger fireplaces, with shelves for storage (especially to keep the salt dry), or with seats, possibly with built-in arm rests. These are cosy inglenooks – the word ingle coming from the Gaelic *aingael*, meaning fire or light. The big fireplace was still used for cooking as well as warmth, so there would be spits and pots and pans hanging about it, and behind the chimney breast a large iron bar ran across the fire, from which were hung sides of bacon or ham for smoking.

One of the troubles with both brick and stone is that they are damaged by heat, so they were protected by ornamental plates or firebacks, which began to appear towards the end of the 16th century, turned out in quantity particularly by the iron foundries in Sussex, often with a date and the Royal Arms cast in. Also in the late 17th century ovens were built into the thick back or the side of the fireplace and closed with a stout wooden shutter or hinged cast iron door (from the 18th century on). These ovens were heated at night – filled with embers from the fire, which were raked out in the morning for bread and pies to be popped in.

Among the other items of fireplace furniture were firedogs, metal supports to stop the large logs from rolling out into the room. Medieval in origin, firedogs were an essential part of the hearth until coal replaced wood as the common fuel.

In 1662, to provide more income for his Exchequer and to help pay for the army, Charles II introduced a Hearth Tax, of two shillings per year for every fireplace, hearth and stove in all but the smallest cottages. It is doubtful whether all of the tax reached the royal coffers, for its collection was put out to freelance agents who were less than scrupulous in their returns. Some agents would mark the main bressumer to show that the house was registered for hearth tax, and these marks can still sometimes be seen. In fact if you can find the listing of the house in the local tax returns for the period you can work out whether the house has been enlarged later by comparing the number of hearths then and now. Although this is far from an infallible guide, for in Essex and other parts of south-east England the fashion evolved of having compound stacks that made it look as if a house had more hearths than it really did: a form of bragging which cost dear when the hearth tax assessor came round. The tax, always unpopular, was repealed at the end of the 17th century.

▨ Regional Fireplace Fashions

As always there are many regional variations from these basic designs. In the stone-bearing regions of Devon and Cornwall, for instance, the usual position of a chimney stack in houses built of stone or cob was on the front wall of the house. It is not as convenient as the axial stack, since its fireplaces only heat two rooms, one on each floor (the hall and the chamber above it). Its position was probably motivated by pride: by putting a new-fangled chimney stack at the front, the owner showed that he was a man of some substance. The chimney was often built in contrasting materials – limestone and sandstone, for example, or in limestone with a chequerwork of flint and stone – further to emphasize its importance.

In the stone-building areas of the Cotswolds, too, the axial stack never became popular and in the Lake District the difficulties of producing squared-off corners using the hard, irregular local stone led to the building of many circular chimney stacks.

The axial stack was not necessarily the only chimney in the house, especially in the larger farmhouses in the south and east of England. Often they would have a second parlour (a forerunner of the dining room) attached to the end of the living room/kitchen, in addition to the parlour at the other side of the central stack. This extra room needed heating too and a small additional fireplace would be built at the gable end.

LATE 17TH CENTURY TO PRESENT DAY

In Tudor, Elizabethan and Jacobean times, each fire had its own chimney top, with individual shafts beautifully decorated, but by the late 17th century the whole stack was being transformed into a solid structure, either square or cruciform in plan, with the flues concealed within it. We can see in these chimneys echoes of classical shapes and patterns, with projecting courses of bricks imitating classical entablature. In this period staircases became the most prominent internal feature of the house and the demand for a grand, central staircase relegated the fireplace again to the edges of the house rather than the middle.

Georgian architects took less interest in the construction of efficient chimneys but devoted their talents to beautifying the fireplaces they served. They reflected the classical design and proportions, embellished often with shouldered decorated architraves supporting the overmantel.

As with most innovations this started with larger houses but it had spread to all types of everyday house by the mid-18th century. In some ways it was a retrogressive step since the central stack helped warm the whole house, but it was permanent: never again was the fireplace to assume a dominating central position in the ordinary home.

In the double-pile house fireplaces were usually built into the end walls, although in eastern England especially it was not uncommon to place them back-to-back on a partition wall.

The Georgian architect faced something of a problem in designing fireplaces and chimney stacks: his buildings followed classical lines, but there were, of course, no classical models of fireplaces for him to follow. As John Woodforde writes in *Georgian Houses for All*: 'Palladio's chimneys had been just tubes put almost anywhere (but unobtrusively) and Georgian builders as though following him in this, took far less interest in the construction of chimneys than their predecessors. But whatever the inadequacy of some Georgian chimney stacks, leading to present-day dampness in bedroom ceilings, much attention was devoted to beautifying the fireplaces they served.' The classical allusions can be seen everywhere in Georgian fireplaces and chimneypieces. More often than not there were mock columns at the sides of the fireplace but even if there were not, the fireplace and chimneypiece's proportions echoed the classical modes, with sections corresponding to base, shaft and capital. The lintel and chimney breast above were modelled on classical entablature.

In large houses, of course, there had been some signs of classical influence as early as the late 16th and early 17th century, but in Wren's time (the late 17th century) the form that found favour was a straightforward surround with a plain bulging moulding, set into oak panelling, known as a 'bolection' moulding. This was followed by a vogue for fireplace surrounds with a shouldered architrave to which might be added decorative scrolls and, to break the long line of the overmantel, a central keystone or tablet.

In the middle Georgian period the typical fireplace had its pilasters, or uprights, surmounted by curved ornamental brackets (consoles) which supported the mantel. A broad mantelshelf was not typical of this period, although it might be added later. As with the other features of the house, the Georgian architect paid great attention to detail in the fireplaces, and precise instructions as to proportions and decorations were laid down in the specifications and the builders' manuals of the time.

The chimney breast in ordinary houses was at first fairly plain with perhaps just one large panel with decorated edges, where a picture could be hung or a mirror fitted. Another popular style was to have three panels, two narrow ones at the sides and a large central one.

A characteristic of the Victorian fireplace was to surround the iron grate with decorative tiles, especially in the best parlour.

The full flowering of Georgian style came in late 18th century fireplaces, notably in the designs of Robert Adam. In the fireplaces of the great houses Neo-classicism was rife, richly-draped female figures, or caryatids or male Atlas figures supporting the mantelshelf, which had now become fairly broad. The less extravagant fireplaces of the everyday house did not aspire to statuary, but were nonetheless well-decorated and ornamented by mouldings, which were mass-produced in a variety of styles by specialist workshops. The most characteristic feature of Adam-style fireplaces was the central plaque, moulded in the most delicate arabesques and scrolling foliage in curving designs.

Marble was the material of choice for early Georgian fireplaces and even those in small houses had marble hearths and surrounds. Later, however, painted wood took over, carved in imitation of the stone prototypes, with added mouldings.

▨ Coal Replaces Wood

One of the reasons why fireplaces could now be so elegant in design and delicate in ornamentation was that they suffered less damage in everyday use,

162

a) 15th century turret

b) 16th century ornate Tudor

c) 17th century square brick

d) 18th century square chimney on Dutch gable

because coal was replacing wood as the common fuel. It had begun to come into domestic use during Tudor times, being brought from the Northumberland coalfields to London and the east coast towns by boat. Because coal was easier to handle and in smaller pieces than logs, the surround was less liable to be knocked about. And since it is slower burning and less is needed, both the fireplace opening and the chimney flue could be narrower. In the old wide chim-

163

neys, cleaning was not too great a problem – a man could get a fair way up and scratch off the soot with a broom of holly leaves. But in the narrower flues, only small boys could squeeze up and generations of tiny chimney sweeps were employed to clean them: a horrifying trade. Some small relief, however, was given to these unfortunate boys by an Act of Parliament in 1840 which set minimum requirements for the width of the flues.

Early grates to hold the coal were tall affairs, placed fairly high in the fireplace opening, with fronts of heavy bowed bars. In the bedrooms and the lesser public rooms, the grate with a hob on the side appeared, the most popular style being the duck's nest grate, the upper semi-circle of bars being supported on a semi-circular arch. Such grates could be in fairly plain cast-iron or in decorated relief echoing the classical details of the principal fireplace.

Chimney pots were most uncommon before the 18th century, although they had been occasionally used as early as the 13th century. It was said that they were introduced to provide a better draught, but they in fact add little to the chimney's efficiency that cannot be achieved by building the stack and flue properly. They were probably first used as a device for adding height to the chimney stacks that protruded from houses with hipped roofs. Such stacks would be unsupported from the level of the eaves upwards and in order to gain the height necessary to avoid down-draughts, a light chimney pot would be added.

It is a curious fact that many Georgian flues were rendered inefficient by the need to keep them out of sight within the thickness of walls: an early example of the dominance of the architect over the craftsman builder. It is not unknown for flues to run horizontally under windows in the 18th century which is hardly conducive to efficiency of smoke removal. Thus chimney pots may also have been needed to help improve the up-draught in houses where there were many fireplaces and a tortuous system of flues, full of curves and angles, but many were necessitated by the switch to coal from timber in existing stacks where the extra height was needed to achieve efficient combustion in a chimney designed for burning wood.

Whatever the reason for introducing chimney pots, they became very popular in the late 18th century and had become standard additions to the chimney stack by Victorian times. They look somewhat incongruous excrescences on the classical outline of the Georgian house and it is quite common to remove them in renovation today. An interesting variation on the chimney pot is a pair of inclined slates resting on the top of the stack, seen particularly in areas like the Lake District. Although these may appear to be ancient, most of them are 19th century.

In the 19th century we first see the development of the Georgian style into

Regency, characterised by lighter designs, and then the move into the Victorian age with its variety of styles and revivals, notably the Gothic, which was reflected in fireplaces as everywhere else inside and outside the house. Many a living room fireplace became florid, fussy and overblown, with solidly carved or turned woodwork, especially in the overmantels. One characteristic style of the Victorian period was to surround the iron grate with decorative tiles. From the 17th century blue Delft style tiles had been used, but the Victorians revelled in their new found skills to produce wonderful and varied tiles, some of which are now collectors pieces, such as those by de Morgan or Minton. After a long period out of fashion, these fireplaces are now once more valued and preserved, in recognition of their period charm and a greater appreciation of the quality of Victorian tile-makers.

In the 19th century kitchen a wide fireplace was still needed to accommodate all the paraphernalia of cooking: the pots and pans and spits and kettles (swung on chains over the open fire). The oven was usually built into the wall at the side of the fireplace and heated independently. By the end of the century, however, the kitchen 'range' was coming in, with a built-in oven and a boiler for heating water. Ranges certainly made cooking easier, and became almost universal in the 19th century, but they did take a lot of fuel to keep the pots boiling, the bread baking and the water bubbling. Ultimately the side boiler of the kitchen range gave way to a back boiler to heat the water, with taps directly to the kitchen sink, and to free-standing gas and electric cookers with their hot plates and ovens.

4

CARING FOR THE HISTORIC HOUSE

Tips and Advice

This section of the book is intended to help owners of old buildings spot problems, get the right advice and try to assess the skill and experience (or otherwise) of builders and agents.

One of the biggest problems that can face the owner of an old property is knowing whether the people who say they can do a job do in fact possess the right skills. No doubt much of what follows applies to all types of buildings and one should bear in mind that any building work, being labour-intensive, is expensive. Appointing the wrong builder or agent can, however, prove considerably more expensive in the long term, so be warned.

A house is the most expensive purchase any of us make in our lives and cutting corners, whether in an old house or a new, is like putting a wooden wheel on a car or a plastic leg on a Chippendale chair. So, good advice is essential. Most local councils have a Conservation Officer, usually in their planning department, who will be pleased to give practical advice. Usually he or she will be happy to visit your house and will often have lists of builders and craftsmen, architects and agents who have done satisfactory work on old buildings.

Try not to pick builders or agents with a pin in Yellow Pages. If you have to, ask them for examples of work they have done; go and look and if possible talk to the house owner. Ask the builder whether he specialises in work on old buildings; whether he does the work himself or sub-contracts it out (which can be a problem); and ask for references from architects or surveyors. Don't be embarrassed to ask: it is your money and your investment you are looking after.

Despite appearances, building work is very specialised and work on old buildings even more so. It is worth appointing an agent, perhaps a surveyor who specialises in conservation work, who will often more than earn his fee by supervising the work to ensure it is done properly. He may well prove more effective than a house owner in getting bad work re-done. Too many building owners hope they can save money by using a general builder and no surveyor, but this can be very much a false economy: bodged work can be very expensive to make good and original fabric may have been unnecessarily destroyed. And remember anyone can set themselves up as a builder with no skills whatsoever: we have all heard stories of cowboy builders. They do the profession no good at all and it is wise to be cautious.

Skill costs money but on the positive side many works proposed for old buildings are unnecessary. For example repointing the brickwork is very rarely needed: perhaps in one case in ten at most, and then only in small areas. Your local Conservation Officer can often save you money by advising against this or other needless expense, including forming damp courses in houses that never had them and do not need them now. Then there are the 'never paint your house again' merchants and other purveyors of zero maintenance. Again, more harm than good. Whatever anyone says there is no such thing as a maintenance-free material or house. Routine maintenance is the key to avoiding major expenditure, as well as knowing what to look for and when to call in the experts.

Thus this section is not intended to make the reader an expert in carrying out building repairs: this book is not a manual for house repairers. The subject is far too specialised and to be effective above a maintenance and redecoration level requires experience and resources. There are jobs and repairs that the owner can do, such as stripping black paint off oak beams, overhauling sash windows and redecorating them, but repairs to timber frames, thatching, pointing, lime plastering and rendering and other jobs are skilled ones that are best left to skilled practitioners.

A further caveat: many old buildings are statutorily listed by the government as being of special architectural or historic interest and special consent is required for any alterations that affect that interest. Again, talk to your local Conservation Officer who will be able to tell you whether what you have in mind requires consent plus give lots of other useful advice. Bear in mind that it is a criminal offence to alter a listed building without consent and bad repairs or replacement of original materials by substitutes like plastic windows and gutters could land an owner in serious trouble. The moral: always ask, the advice is free and willingly given by enthusiasts who love old buildings.

▨ ROOF PROBLEMS ▨

The purpose of the roof is to keep water out of the building. Thus when a roof fails to do this and the problem is not spotted very costly repairs may be needed. Always keep a weather eye on the roof. If a slate slips or a tile breaks, water will find the hole and pour in. If the thatch erodes, water will get in. If you have lead valley or parapet gutters a pin hole in the lead could lead to timber decay, hidden from sight. So the best thing to do is look at your roof on a regular basis. If you see a problem get the builder in to replace the missing tile or slate, or the thatcher to remake the ridge or patch as needed. This routine maintenance approach will almost certainly save you a great deal of money: 'a stitch in time saves nine' applies to buildings just as much as clothing.

169

Damp is indeed the main enemy of roofs, as of the house at large for it not only attacks the roof covering but in time can lead to a serious deterioration of the supporting timbers and could eventually cause the roof to collapse.

▓ Thatch

While water reed roofs should last a lifetime and more (up to a hundred years for Norfolk reed), their poor relation, long straw thatch, has a service life of only some twenty five years. The more woody combed wheat reed should last for about fifty years, but normally the softer material, usually rye straw, needed for the ridge requires attention more frequently. You can expect to re-ridge perhaps every twenty years or so, sometimes less. This will probably necessitate a rewiring as well, unless the wire netting cover is in good enough condition to allow it to be reused.

Thatch is a natural material and susceptible to the climate and its immediate environs. Overhanging trees and the damp conditions they can cause accelerate decay, so if you can keep trees away from a thatched roof all the better. The signs of deterioration are easy enough to spot: the roof will look rather patchy and uneven, and moss patches will indicate areas of trouble. Perhaps the most conclusive of evidence is patches of damp in the ceilings below the thatch.

A rule of thumb for deciding whether repair is necessary is when the thatch has eroded sufficiently for the 'liggers' (the hazel thatch pins) to stick up well above the surface of the thatch: a particular problem at the ridges. Erosion of the thatch away from the chimney or failure of the cement fillets or lead dressings can be spotted by the house owner.

However, thatching is a skilled craft and repair or replacement can only be done by an expert thatcher. Again, your local authority Conservation Officer should have a list of local thatchers or can put you in touch with the local representative of the Master Thatchers association.

▓ Tiles, Slates and Stone

Slipped or missing tiles, slates or stone slabs are, of course, the tell-tale signs of problems with these roofing materials and the cause of the trouble is usually the corrosion or perishing of the fixing pegs or nails, or the failure of the battens onto which the covering is fastened. Frost and general erosion can also cause slates and tiles to split and crack. Ironically the modern obsession with roofing felt has caused the decay of many roofs. If the felt is not allowed to sag well between the rafters condensation builds up under the slate or tile and this leads to accelerated erosion and decay! Felt is of course of assistance if there is heavy, driving snow but the benefit of a well ventilated roof space is lost.

170

A patch repair may be all that is needed, removing the damaged or slipped tiles, slates or flags, making good the battens, and renailing or pegging the coverings. Tiles may be re-hung on oak pegs or with copper, aluminium alloy, or stainless steel nails: galvanised nails are regarded as risky for the hammering needed to fix them can fracture the galvanising and open the door to rust.

Make sure your specialist roofing contractor keeps all the original tiles or slates that are still roof-worthy, and wherever possible, find similar old tiles or slates for the replacements. Be suspicious if he says he cannot salvage any, for this is an extremely rare situation: he may wish to sell the salvaged ones!

Nothing looks worse than an old roof patched with modern materials, and indeed a modern roof (concrete tile, for example) on an old house leaves much to be desired. Original materials are scarce, but well worth searching for. The yards of demolition contractors are often a fruitful place to begin, or local farmers might be persuaded to part with tiles, slates or stone flags from tumbledown barns or sheds. However, first make sure that the barns are not listed buildings and bear in mind that any change in materials on a listed house requires listed building consent.

While you can replace the odd slipped or missing slate or tile, anything more should be left to a specialist roofing contractor.

Gutters

Faulty guttering or leaking downpipe joints are common problems in the older house and can lead to damp penetration, particularly along the tops of walls. In many cases, however, the old gutter may not be leaking due to damage but be overflowing because of some blockage.

Cast iron and zinc guttering can be repaired with mastic materials although generally this proves to be a temporary 'patch up' solution. Replacement cast iron rainwater goods are widely available now, thanks to the conservation movement, and will outlast any plastic substitutes. Government advice on listed buildings makes clear that cast iron is the appropriate material and consent is very unlikely for plastic on a listed building, a material which is in any case inappropriate for an old building.

Roof Supports

Once water has breached the outer defences and reached the roof supports, deterioration is not far away. Fungus infections soon bring rotting, and wood-devouring beetles thrive in damp conditions. Signs of trouble are, from the outside, hollows in the pitched part of the roof and sagging or undulations along the ridge; and from within the roof-space, a musty smell, crumbling wood and the flight-holes of the beetles.

171

Early remedial action can be taken by the householder himself; but if major replacement of timbers (particularly structural ones) is required, or rampant rot or worm need eliminating, specialists must be called in. Both wet rot and dry rot are fungus infections. Dry rot is the most deadly cause of serious damage in old buildings.

Whatever the size of the timbers or quality of the wood, regular inspection and prompt remedial action will repay the effort. Many old cottages do not have loft hatches so the roof space cannot be inspected, and it is well worth investing in having one installed.

Treatment should begin, as always, by eliminating the cause: repairing, for instance, the roof covering where the damp has penetrated. All timber affected by dry rot should be cut away and renewed. After repairs, fungicide should be applied to remaining timbers, the new wood and brickwork, masonry and walling, to kill any residual spores and to prevent further attacks of rot.

'Wet rot' is an umbrella title applied to other fungi, which generally do not pose so great a problem since they cannot spread to sound timber. Wet rot may cause deep cracks along a timber's grain, but the 'cubing' effect of dry rot is seldom seen. Treatment is to cut away and replace affected timbers and spray with fungicide.

▨ Beetle

Beetle infestation is generally described as 'woodworm', and that is fair enough, for the damage is caused by the larvae, or worms, of the beetle chewing their way through the wood. Although they make unsightly and rather worrying flight holes as they emerge, woodworm attack is rarely as serious as fungal decay.

Death-watch beetle have a preference for (damp) hardwoods, while the furniture beetle can be found in both sappy hardwoods and softwoods, and are a more serious pest in post-medieval houses. Here softwood and sapwood (the outer parts of the tree) began to replace the earlier use of mainly harder heartwoods of oak.

Death-watch beetle can normally only attack damp hardwoods: they do not have steel teeth. If you have an outbreak there is a reason. Yet again, damp is the cause. The exit holes are larger for death-watch than woodworm, and the damage can be more extensive inside the timber. The trick to find out whether the infestation is active or long defunct is to examine the bore holes carefully, looking for those that seem fresh and have traces of bore dust around them.

Woodworm can be effectively treated with a number of proprietary preparations especially formulated for the job, which are sprayed into the timber. Treatment is best left to the experts as most of the chemicals are dangerous and it is important to choose a firm which enjoys a good local, or even national, reputation.

If an ancient roof looks to be sagging or misshapen, however, it does not necessarily need repair. Building was normally done using 'green' or new oak timbers which then matured after the house was built, twisting and warping to alter their shape and shift the structure. This is why many old houses look a little bent and buckled even though they are perfectly sound. The temptation to straighten them out should be resisted as this could actually cause serious damage to the structure.

WALL PROBLEMS

The ivy-covered wall has long been regarded as a traditional feature of older properties. Charming it may be, but it can do the wall little good, attacking the mortar between the joints and even pushing brickwork apart and roof tiles off. Naturalists like it, of course, so if you do as well, keep it under control and trimmed.

Ivy is, however, a relatively minor problem for walls. Others with far more potentially serious effects include settlement and the deterioration of wall fabric.

Settlement

Settlement is the result of the ground having given way or subsided beneath the wall so the foundation is no longer sufficiently firm. The collapse of old mine workings, the diversion of a spring or underground stream, the ever-probing roots of adjacent trees, or even the washing away of the ground by a blocked downpipe or failed drainpipe can cause settlement in a wall that has otherwise been standing safely for centuries.

It is difficult to cure and its diagnosis and treatment are best left to experts. The normal approach these days is to underpin the affected wall by excavating new foundations and forming a concrete foundation to support the wall. However, with old lime mortar walls it may be possible to back fill locally and rebuild 'soft' foundations to reduce the risk of differential settlement occurring between the rest of the house and the new heavy and rigid concrete underpinning usually adopted.

Clearly expertise is needed and you must ask for professional advice from a surveyor or structural engineer but, and this is crucial, make sure he or she is a specialist in historic building work. Most are trained to deal with modern buildings which work in a completely different way structurally, so you need an advisor who understands historic construction and is prepared to think imaginatively

173

and conservatively. English Heritage, the Government's advisor on heritage matters, has a simple rule: the Two Day Rule, which should be a source of great comfort to the owners of historic buildings – 'If it's here today, it'll be here tomorrow'.

Indeed, settlement is less of a problem to an old building than to a new one which has rigid foundations and brickwork with hard Portland cement mortar. Look at old buildings: they can lean drunkenly, sag, tilt and bow but they survive, if left well alone. Many settled soon after they were built, so you must ask for expert, sympathetic advice.

▨ Deterioration of the Wall Fabric

The wall's basic task is to keep out the weather, and it is the weather that is the wall's greatest enemy. Different types of walling, however, fail in rather different ways:

Clay wall problems: To maintain their solidity and coherence, clay walls must be kept dry; so their 'boots', the damp-resisting brick or stone base on which they are raised, must continue to be effective, the 'overcoat' of rendering should be maintained intact, and the 'hat', the roof, must keep water off the tops of the walls. A cob wall has to have a certain level of moisture within it to ensure it remains intact, but excessive damp funnelled through cracks in the render, missing tiles at the top of the wall or soil build-up over the base causes the material to erode away or turn back into mud.

The house owner should ensure that garden beds do not build up above the stone or brick base, that cracks in the render are swiftly repaired and missing tiles made good. Never be persuaded to insert a damp course into any cob wall. Like all traditional walling the moisture level is critical and moisture needs to be able to escape into the ground as part of the natural wet/dry cycle in dealing with weather. A damp course stops this and can lead to accumulation of moisture in the lower part of the wall above the impermeable damp course and to a subsequent failure of the cob.

Make sure your contractor knows what he is doing and that the render is a sand lime one: more than the merest whiff of cement in the mix will stop the wall 'breathing'. If repairs are needed to internal plaster on the walls, again this must be a porous mix, not a rock-hard water-proofing one which will trap moisture behind it.

Timber wall problems: Although timber itself is not greatly weakened merely by being damp, the evils of wet and dry rot flourish in damp conditions (see Roofs for details) and prompt remedial treatment is recommended.

174

To protect the timber frame the insertion of a damp proof course in the supporting dwarf wall or plinth may be helpful between the wall and the timber sole plate. Indeed, the sole plate is often the most vulnerable timber in the building and should be regularly inspected. It can be replaced if completely rotted away by a new one, either green oak or second-hand. Most specialist builders use green oak and their views should be respected. The use of second-hand timber tends to be merely a desire to match the rest of the frame, but this is not necessary. Best practice is to use green oak. Again, however, this is very much a job for a specialist in timber-frame repairs, not a general builder: the local Conservation Officer should be able to help with a few names here.

Where the panels between the studs are of wattle and daub, these may have deteriorated in the course of time and become unstable. They are a valuable (and efficiently insulating) part of the building's history and expert specialist builders should be consulted for their repair.

Brick and stone wall problems: In an older building the mortar is intended to be softer than the surrounding brick or stone. Thus the mortar sacrifices itself for the wall. The great tragedy of the 20th century has been the indiscriminate use of hard Portland cement mortars for pointing between the bricks and stones of walls. Weather always takes the easy option and attacks the softer material, so accelerated decay of the wall is the product of hard cementitious mortar: the ubiquitous mix of one part of cement to three parts of sand.

In historic buildings lime mortar should always be used and if you are tempted to do a little pointing yourself take expert advice: the local Conservation Officer will be able to advise you of appropriate mortar mixes.

Repointing, as was stated earlier, is needed far less frequently than many believe. Until the pointing has worn back at least an inch from the face of the brick or stone it is a waste of time and, more importantly, money.

Obviously if running water or similar problems cause washing out of the mortar or turn it back into sand, localised repointing is required and eventually complete repointing is needed. However, house owners should avoid a temptation to repoint merely to make the place look spick and span: 18th and 19th century lime mortar was of high quality and beautiful to look at. Alas most modern pointing, except by conservation specialists, is very bad indeed. The mix is almost always full of hard cement, too wet, the sand too yellow and the pointing technique unhistoric 'bucket handle' or worse 'weathered', 'snail-creep' or 'ribbon'. Let the wrong builder loose on your house and you can ruin its appearance, for pointing is a vital element in its appearance, quite apart from leading to accelerated decay of your brick or stone work.

▨ Internal Walls

Internal walls from the late 16th century onwards were often covered with plaster, laid on laths attached to battens. These unfortunately occasionally require attention due to failure of the fixing nails or the depredations of rot and woodworm. Sometimes the loss of battens may be immaterial, as in the centre of mouldings and covings, as they were often no longer needed for support once the plaster had set. When battens in long flat areas are lost or damaged, however, there may be sagging, bowing and crumbling of the plaster.

Wholesale replacement of the batten and lath base is often not necessary, for weak areas can be strengthened in a variety of ways, using counter-sunk brass cups and screws for instance. Batten channels can be dug away to provide a key for a fresh coat of plaster, reinforced by a hessian or metal mesh backing.

Replacement of traditional lath and plaster by modern plasterboard seems a beguiling and cheap option, but should be avoided in a listed building or by any owner who cares about his or her historic house. A specialist plasterer able to work with traditional methods and materials should be used. In any case, if your house is a listed building, the change from lath and plaster to plasterboard would require prior consent from your Council.

▨ WINDOW REPAIR AND RESTORATION ▨

As with many other parts of the house, the main cause of trouble with windows is damp. A regular protective coat of paint is the answer, to prevent the damp penetrating into the wood and setting up the conditions for rot to develop. If repainted every four or five years, a well made timber window will last for a considerable time, possibly indefinitely. Since paint itself is attacked by sunlight and by heat, particular attention should be paid to south-facing windows.

Examine your windows regularly for signs of paint peeling away or chipping off. If the damage is slight, all that will be needed is a smoothing off with glasspaper and a new top coat applied. With more extensive flaking and peeling it is better to strip back to the wood, either by burning off the paint or by using a proprietary paint stripper, and then apply at least three good protective layers, of primer, undercoat and top coat.

A popular fad these days is to strip the paintwork and stain the wood or to stain replacement windows. This is only appropriate in oak or other traditional hardwood windows. For softwoods it is unhistoric and is usually done in ginger or dark brown: the effect is to change the appearance of the building so that its 'eyes', that is its windows, are blanked out. The secret of success in painting is to do it properly on decent wood. It is slightly more difficult now as lead has been banned from paint. This acted as a preservative and helped paint adhere.

Most factory-made windows these days are kiln dried and paint does not stick as well as it should. However, on old windows which were made with seasoned timber paint should stick better. Staining is yet another example of trying to reduce maintenance. If you are determined to stain use a white opaque one which at least goes some way to simulating the traditional appearance and finish of softwood windows which were invariably painted.

Restoration

If the previous owners were less than fastidious in the protection of their exterior woodwork there will almost certainly be some deterioration of the wood through rotting. It is not possible to make this sound and the only sensible course is to remove the rotten area and replace it. Where the damage is really extensive, it is better, despite the cost, to remove and replace the whole window frame.

In old houses this can prove to be an expensive business, especially if the original windows are of a unique and sophisticated design. A replica will have to be made up by a professional joiner so that the new window is in keeping with the others. Ready-made window frames can be bought in all shapes and sizes, but most mass-produced frames tend to be heavier and clumsier than earlier hand-crafted ones and look terribly out of place. It is also extremely rare to need to replace more than a few windows or parts of windows. If a builder (or, perish the thought, a double-glazing salesman) says all your windows are 'shot', get a second opinion. Only after many years of utter dereliction is total replacement ever going to be likely. For many lazy or under-trained builders it is easier to replace than repair, as the latter needs skills that a depressingly large number of builders conspicuously lack.

Incidentally, if your house is a listed building, then you cannot make a change in window frames without obtaining consent from your local authority planning department. In any case ask its Conservation Officer for advice.

Window sills

Window sills are generally made of hardwood, and tend to be more durable than the rest of the frame. They need to be, of course, because they take the brunt of the water. Check them regularly, for damage, particularly underneath, not only to make sure the paint looks sound but also, by pressing with the thumb, to feel if the wood has gone spongy. The sill has a groove or 'drip' underneath, to keep the water away from the wall, so make sure this has not become clogged with paint and muck.

If there is not a great deal of decay, the sill could be renovated by a dressing sheet of lead. Localised rot can be cured by cutting away the offending area and

177

grafting in a new piece of hardwood before repainting. However, if the damage is extensive, it is better to remove and replace the whole sill.

There can be problems with the internal sills too, particularly in old houses where central heating has been installed. The warm dry air can cause the wood to shrink, creating a gap between window frame and sill. There are many proprietary plastic fillers on the market today which should overcome subsequent problems of shrinking and cracking.

▨ Sash and Sliding Windows

Sash and sliding windows are often belittled by salesmen, but maintenance is all that is needed to keep them functioning smoothly. A build up of several layers of paint has two effects: it makes the windows hard to move and upsets the balance of the weights. Thus it is probably better practice to take the sash out and strip the old paint off before repainting. Check the counterweights and add extra weight if the sash is now heavier. The sliding sash is a wonderful device and the wise historic home owner ignores the siren voices telling him or her that they are draughty and inefficient.

The commonest complaint is that they stick – a fault to which Yorkshire sashes are particularly prone, especially during a wet season when the wood expands. A bit of candle wax in the channels often works, otherwise the only remedy is to take out the sliding section and carefully smooth away small amounts of wood so that the window will glide easily in its channels. Repainting any bits of exposed wood will stop further water penetration.

Vertical sliding sashes also run into mechanical problems. All too familiar is the breaking of the sash cord.

If you are no handyman, it might be advisable to get someone professional to do the job, for it can be a little tricky – and frustrating.

▨ Reglazing

If you have to replace the windows, always save the old glass and use it in the new frames. Crown glass particularly should be conserved, as it is irreplaceable and its slight imperfections add much to the character of a window. Make sure your builder understands your instructions: broken glass cannot be reassembled.

Double glazing presents a dilemma for the owner of an old house. It obviously makes sense to cut back on heating bills by eliminating draughts and reducing heat loss. Our own inclination, if the old windows in the house are sound, is not to double glaze but to concentrate on roof insulation and making sure the windows are draught-free. They are likely to be smaller than modern ones so heat loss should be less.

178

There are many double glazing systems on the market, but again ignore the siren voices saying they look the same as the original windows. Very, very few do and these are expensive. They are the sort that are manufactured by companies or craftsmen that do not need to employ teams of high pressure salesmen! Double glazing only reduces outside noise by 3 decibels: a barely perceptible improvement. It is the draught stripping that keeps noise out and this can be applied to single glazed windows equally effectively.

Your local council's Conservation Officer can give advice that often saves you unnecessary expense and in the case of listed buildings the Government's advice is clear: double glazing is inappropriate. It is likely that the Conservation Officer will suggest a secondary glazing system that does not affect the original window and is reversible.

Opening Up Old Windows

Second only to the joy of discovery and opening up an old fireplace is the restoration of an old blocked-up window. In timber-framed houses particularly, the original mullions of a blocked-up window will probably still be there, even though the window frame has been plastered over, or filled in with wattle and daub or brick. Restoring a window and glazing it sensitively will add a very pleasing feature to the house, and give some sense of its original appearance.

We said earlier that windows are a house's eyes, they add so much to its character. So it is vital in window restoration or replacement to proceed with the greatest care. If you have any doubts, consult an architect with experience in restoration or get in touch with your local council's Planning Department whose Conservation Officer should have plenty of practical (and money saving) advice.

FLOOR REPAIR PROBLEMS

The new owner of an old house may well find that his floors are worn and decayed. Earthen floors have all but disappeared, covered over with brick and tile, but even these more substantial coverings are subject to wear and tear, especially where there has been a heavy passage of feet over the years. Before ripping up an old floor, however, and replacing it with a modern damp-proofed concrete base, it is wise to pause for thought. Fitted carpets over concrete can be perfectly in keeping with an old house, but nothing can enhance it more than having at least a principal room or two floored in traditional materials.

One of the delights of ancient floor tiles – and old bricks, too – was that they were hand-made; it is their subtle variations in colour that give old floors such a pleasing look. Modern machine-made floor tiles are uniform, so this effect is lost; and even replacing only the very worn or broken old tiles with new ones is

179

seldom a satisfactory solution. It is worth asking local builders or demolition contractors for old tiles, but there is a heavy demand for them and they are difficult to find. The answer for floor renovation, however, could lie literally beneath your feet, for you may find that all you need to do is take up the tiles and turn them over. The undersides of old tiles are often surprisingly well preserved and it is worth examining this possibility before opting for a complete modern replacement floor in tile or concrete.

Another approach where there are many broken or very badly worn tiles is to make a concrete floor in the centre of the room, which can be covered with a rug or small carpet, and surround it with whatever tiles can be saved.

Whenever a tile floor has to be relaid the opportunity should be taken to damp-proof, by excavating and putting in an under-layer of concrete incorporating a damp-proof membrane. Damp is of course often a major problem in timber floors at ground level, the particularly vulnerable areas being where the floorboards meet the walls. Many timber floors are supported on joists laid directly on the ground and these joists are, not surprisingly, particularly vulnerable to wet rot. Regular inspection, including if necessary taking up damaged boards, is vital so that remedial action can be taken as quickly as possible. (Details of treatment and cure of rot and worm damage are given on p 172.) To prevent rot it is essential to have the floorboards as well ventilated as possible and airbricks in the walls below floor level are essential.

People tend to worry more about the state of their upper floors, imagining that bed or bath are likely to come tumbling through to the floor below. In fact upper floors are less susceptible to damp than those near ground level, except where the joists and beams socket into the outside walls. The best first test of its soundness is simply to jump up and down on it a few times (perhaps gently!). If it gives rather too much and bounces back sluggishly, there may well be worm attack to the joists. If you cannot see these from below, then prise up a few boards to see what is going on. (You may have to remove the skirting board first.) Look carefully at joists and the undersides of the boards for signs of infestation. If all seems well, you can nail back the boards, but if there is any worm damage, the wisest course is to take up all the boards. Mark them with chalk so that they can be fitted back in the same position. If the infestation is not too bad it will just be a question of cutting away and replacing the odd areas of worm damage or rot, but joists showing a lot of damage should be replaced.

Where there is only a little infestation give it a good going-over with a wire brush. Next apply a couple of coats of an all-purpose fungicide/insecticide/wood preservative, all over the joists and other timbers, and on the undersides of the floorboards. Replace the boards and nail into position, sweep clean and paint them over with a mixture of wood stain and preservative. The back of the skirting boards should be treated with preservative too before being nailed home.

If worm or rot damage is really bad, or if there are distinct structural problems then it is really best to call in an expert, who will know of sophisticated techniques for reinforcing floors. Some of these techniques are detailed in a pamphlet 'Strengthening Timber Floors', available from the Society for the Protection of Ancient Buildings.

▦ STAIRCASE PROBLEMS ▦

It is most important that the stairs in an old house are kept in good condition, since worn and broken stairs can be dangerous and even deadly. Treads and risers, usually made of softwood, are particularly susceptible to rot and worm infestation and should therefore be inspected regularly, looking particularly for penetrating damp if the stairs run against an outside wall. Worm damage can be spotted easily if the undersides of the treads and risers are accessible, but often they are covered over, by lath and plaster for instance, so a more careful inspection of the upper surfaces is called for. To prevent rot it helps to have the space beneath the ground or basement floor staircase adequately ventilated to keep the damp at bay.

Stairs are also subject to wear and to mechanical instability caused by shrinkage of the treads and risers or by settlement of the supporting structure. All this will almost certainly lead to creaks and in later stages could be downright dangerous. Look out for tell-tale gaps between surfaces which should fit snugly together. The adjustment of the staircase using wedges or tie rods should not be beyond the skills of the house owner, provided that the structure is not too complicated, but a skilled carpenter will be needed for the finer assemblies.

The balusters and newels of staircases have often been killed by kindness, by layer upon layer of paint obscuring the fine carved work. If you can find the time all old paint should be stripped off and the wood freshly painted. Handrails, particularly, were often made of mahogany, oak or another good hardwood, and covering them over with paint is a tragedy. While humbler pine balusters and handrails should be painted, hardwood handrails should be stripped of paint and polished or varnished.

▦ FIREPLACE PROBLEMS ▦

In a house built before the 18th century the original fireplaces will probably have been drastically altered since – converted from wood to coal-burning, for instance, or filled with a Victorian or modern grate and surround. The original fireplace, even perhaps with an inglenook, may still be there, hidden behind the

181

'improvements' and it can be exposed to its former glory with a little time and effort.

The first job is to locate the original fireplace lintel or bressumer, which will most likely be somewhere above the top of the replacement fireplace. In many conversions to coal-burning the lintel was left exposed, but equally in many others it was completely plastered over. If there are no signs of it (look for the outline of its shape beneath wall paint or paper), then the only thing to do is to dig for it, probing carefully into the plaster. Once found, and the surrounding plaster scraped away, the lintel's condition should be carefully examined. If it is not perfectly sound, it may need to be repaired or replaced by a similar baulk of timber: a job very much best left to a specialist builder.

More often than not the solid oak beam will be whole and sound, and the laborious and dusty task of removing the newer fireplace can begin. There may be an accumulation of several fireplaces of earlier dates behind the modern facade, but with luck the brickwork of the original cavity will soon be exposed. All the mess and rubble should be cleared away and the bricks of the supporting plinths and the side of the fireplace should be cleaned thoroughly by wirebrushing. Nothing looks better in an old house than a cheery wood fire burning in a large original fireplace. However, in today's draught-proofed houses getting a fire to burn well is a problem and solutions include taking in air through an airbrick or two put into the wall of an outside chimney, or by an under-floor conduit from the outside, ending in a grille at or near the hearth. Some such step is needed to create an updraught so smoke goes up the chimney and does not billow out into the room.

Smoking problems

Smoking can be a problem in a newly opened-up chimney, but as well as checking that it is reasonably clean and free from obstructions, other action can be taken to overcome it. The fire can be raised higher in the fireplace opening, either by putting bricks in the base of the firebasket, or by raising the basket itself, supporting its feet on bricks. Alternatively a hood to trap and carry off the smoke can be inserted into the fireplace opening.

Using a firebasket, however, does not solve the problem of fuel consumption and another alternative is to install a cast-iron wood burning stove. These now come in a variety of attractive styles and are increasingly popular in country districts. With them, at least, the hearth and fireplace surround can be seen as they originally were. But perhaps the best answer is to keep the open fire for show or for winter and put in discreet central heating for warmth and comfort. If you decide not to use the fireplace but merely have it as an interesting feature of the room the chimney should be blocked off to prevent heat loss.

For houses built in the 18th and 19th centuries, with coal-burning grates, smoking should not be much of a problem, for by that time many experts had bent their minds to produce better designs.

The appearance of many an 18th and 19th century room has been spoiled by replacing the original grates and surrounds with modern fitted fireplaces. When renovating such a house you may again, as with older houses, like to consider reversing the process: out with the new and back with the old.

▧ CHIMNEY PROBLEMS ▧

The exposed chimney stack is the part most vulnerable to damage and decay. Assaulted on the outside by the weather, it is attacked from within by acid residues in the smoke, which eat into the bricks and mortar.

The weather attacks the chimney structure on two fronts. On the side facing the prevailing wind, driving rain weakens and wears away at the joints between the bricks. The other side away from the wind dries out only slowly, and when the water in and around it freezes and expands in the winter, tensions are set up which tend to make the chimney lean and, ultimately, topple. Chimneys should be examined whenever possible, during other roof work for instance, and repaired as necessary. At the same time the damp-excluding layer where chimney stack meets roof should be checked and renovated.

If damage extends only to the mortar, then repointing is all that is required, trowelling fresh lime mortar into the cracks after they have been carefully raked out. The mortar should be slightly recessed, never proud, and finished off with a brush to bring the harder aggregate in it to the surface. Make sure your builder knows how to point in a way suitable for an old building before you unleash him on such a prominent feature of your house!

For more serious decay, and especially if there are a fair number of cracked or eroded bricks, the only solution is to take down and rebuild the top of the stack, using as many of the original bricks as possible. Old bricks to plug the gaps can probably be found at local builders or demolition contractors.

Before going to the trouble and expense of demolishing and rebuilding, however, and particularly if the stack is an ornate one, consider the possibility of *in situ* repairs. There are a number of clever specialised techniques for strengthening stacks from the inside.

Chimney pots, made of baked clay, are less weather-resistant than the main stack and will wear or crack more quickly. The squared pots of white clay which became popular in the Georgian and Regency period were difficult to replace, but firms like Red Bank now produce and keep a huge range of chimney pots, so quick and easy replacement should be possible.

183

An alternative, though, is to remove the damaged pots altogether: many chimney pots are later additions to old property and not an integral part of the original design. Another option is to swap the damaged pots in prominent positions with sounder ones from less conspicuous places. Chimney stacks which are no longer used should be capped off to stop the rain coming in, but ventilation is vital to prevent the build-up of damp in the flue.

∽ 5 ∽

HOW TO DATE
A HOUSE

When Was It Built?

▨ INTRODUCTION ▨

The aim of this section of the book is to provide a simple technique for identifying and dating with a fair degree of accuracy the old houses in our towns and villages and in the countryside. By answering a few straightforward questions about the houses you are looking at, you will be able to 'home in' on their type, style and date.

You will, however, be judging by external appearance and it is entirely possible and indeed, quite likely that the face a house shows to the world will be much younger than the bones beneath. Many old houses had new facades imposed upon them and had their windows, doors and decorative features altered as owners sought to modernise their properties and keep up with prevailing fashions. It is often possible to find out more about the original building by looking at the sides and back of a house, which may have been altered less, and at such basic attributes as the depth of the house, the height of the storeys and the pitch of the roof.

For the church and the grand country house, style and decorative features enable experts to date building and re-building with great accuracy (to say nothing of the help they receive from documentary evidence, so often conspicuously lacking for the smaller house). For the everyday house, such precise dating is not so easy, because the timing of the introduction of new formats and features and of their abandonment varies greatly, due to a number of factors.

First, there is geographical location. As a general rule new ideas were introduced in the south-east of England and spread slowly northwards and westwards. It could be many, many decades before a new style penetrated to the more remote areas, by which time it could well have been superseded in its place of origin. There are, however, many exceptions to the general geographical rule, one of the most striking being East Anglia which was innovative and influential in the Middle Ages, but later declined when the prosperous wool trade of the area ended.

Secondly, the size or status of a building often determined the use of novel features; they occur first in larger houses and only later are used in smaller ones, in cottages and in farm buildings. In addition, more conservative local builders continued to use older styles and features many years after more progressive ones had moved on to the new, so buildings in different styles, even in the same area, may date from the same period.

Nonetheless, most of us with a passing interest in old houses do not normally want to date them with the precision of an expert. We are content with a fair idea of their age and style. Working your way through this section will enable you to achieve just that.

First, to get a 'feel' for the house in front of you, ask a few basic questions...

▨ SOME BASIC QUESTIONS ▨

1. Where is it?

In towns and villages, older houses tend to be in the centre, near the church and market place. Outer suburbs tend to be a later development, although they sometimes absorb older villages. Street names, e.g. George Street, Waterloo Place, Sebastopol Villas can help, too, for they often commemorate contemporary events. Look out for Georgian rectories, Victorian villas.

Farmhouses in the countryside might be Tudor in some parts of the country, but in the Midlands and East Anglia, the country of the nucleated village set in its open fields for example, they will usually be later, after 17th and 18th century Enclosure Acts divided up the open fields and farmsteads were built in the middle of the new land holdings.

2. How tall are the storeys?

The general rule is the older the house, the lower the storeys. Jettying (protruding upper storeys) appears in the 15th century and continued into the mid 17th century.

In the 18th and 19th centuries it was common for the front and back walls to be raised and the roof flattened, giving more upper floor headroom. Look for tell-tale signs of new work, especially at the gable ends. Sometimes only the front was raised and the rear of the roof retains its original steeper pitch.

3. How deep is the house?

Most smaller houses were only one room deep until the 18th century. Then the two room deep (double pile) plan became popular, although the single room deep small house and cottage continued into the 20th century. Earlier double pile houses may have an M-shaped roof. Later the roof spans the whole depth. Look for later additions to earlier shallower houses.

4. How steep is the roof?

Up to the 15th century, most smaller houses were thatched, except where thin local stone or slate was available. Thatched roofs would be steeply pitched (45 to 55 degrees, even steeper if long-straw was used) to allow rainwater to flow off. Stone, slate and pantile roofs have shallower pitches. Tiles or slates may replace thatch on older steeper roofs. Look for telltale signs of an original thicker covering around chimney stacks and inside gables: perhaps a cement fillet or a stone drip parallel to and higher than the existing roof covering.

5. Is the main elevation symmetrical?
A symmetrical facade suggests the late 17th century and beyond. It may be a remodelling. Check the chimney stacks: they are difficult to re-site, so asymmetry suggests a new facade.

Answers to these questions will have provided some basic clues to the age of the house. For more precise identification we need to look at the materials used and at some of the finer details.

▦ WHAT IS IT BUILT OF? ▦
1. Is it built of timber?
Timber was the commonest material for everyday houses from medieval times, except in those areas where local stone was easily accessible. Few ordinary timber houses built before the 15th century survive, and these are usually homes of the better-off farmers, yeomen and merchants.

The earliest houses have large timber frames, strengthened with various braces, but from the mid-15th century in the north and west, and the late 16th elsewhere, smaller panels took over. Close vertical studding was popular, in the south-east especially in the 16th and early 17th centuries.

The shortage of good timber from the later 17th century led to the use of lighter and rougher timbers, covered with rendering, weatherboarding or tiles. Fire hazards and legislation combined with the arrival of cheaper brick and building stone meant the virtual end of timber-frame house building by the early 18th century; except for farm buildings where an early 19th century one may still have timber-framing of as high a quality as in the 17th century.

Problems with dating timber houses come from the ease of alteration and from the fact that old timbers were frequently re-used, often descending the social scale in the process: the better off could afford new timber. Also watch out for 'fakes' where an old 'feel' is deliberately created using ancient timbers, which may have no structural function.

For further details turn to pages 191 to 195.

2. Is it built of stone?

Some notable examples of stone houses from the 12th century onwards still remain, such as the town houses of rich merchants or stone-built country hall houses. In areas where workable stone was readily available there has been a long tradition of stone building, even for smaller houses, although elsewhere they were uncommon until the 16th and 17th centuries.

By the 17th century, good quality small stone houses were being built in the Cotswolds and in other areas such as the south-west, although they were rare in the poorer areas of the north until the mid-17th century.

Flints and cobbles were also used as walling material, usually strengthened with stonework and, later, with brick dressings at the angles, around openings and to the eaves and the plinth, and often had bands between storeys.

Building techniques varied widely, according to the nature of the material, although generally the bigger stones were laid at the base and better quality stones were used for the quoins and around windows and doors. Rougher stone was used elsewhere and then covered with limewash (often removed in the 19th century when there was a fashion for bare stone) or disguised with rendering.

Ashlar, a fine quality stone cut into rectangular blocks, was typical of high-quality Georgian building, although again cheaper, rougher-hewn stone was frequently used and rendered over. The 19th century saw the last period of widespread stone use before cheap transport made brick universally available.

Dating of smaller stone houses can be difficult, because the same building methods were used for centuries, and in general more attention needs to be paid to architectural features than to the building techniques themselves.

For more details, turn to pages 195 to 197.

3. Is it built of brick?

Bricks were little used in everyday houses before the 15th century, but the great rebuilding of the 16th and 17th centuries saw their increasingly widespread use. They were used first in the south and east and spread gradually throughout the country, first in better-class houses (replacing timber-framing and clay walls) and later in smaller ones.

By the late 17th century small brick houses were more common and brick use was widespread in the 18th. Many timber and clay houses were refaced with brick in this period. Bricks were also used to replace wattle and daub panel infilling: a cheaper modernisation than rebuilding the whole house.

Brick taxes (introduced in 1784 and finally abolished in 1850) encouraged production of larger bricks and the use of weatherboarding and imitation bricks, but mass production and cheap transport made bricks the universal construction material in the 19th century.

Early hand-made bricks were irregular in size and required more mortar in the joints; 19th century machine-made bricks were more regular and joints could be thinner.

Clues for the dating of brick buildings can also come from the colour of the bricks and from the patterns (bonds) in which they are laid. For more details turn to pages 197 to 198.

4. Is it made of clay or rendered over?

Clay was used as a walling material from the earliest times up to the 18th and 19th centuries. Cob, a mixture of clay and straw built up in layers, is typical of Devon, but similar techniques were used in the Midlands, Wales and the North-West. In East Anglia, clay lumps or bats were used: the clay/straw mixture being moulded into large oblong blocks. By the 19th century many clay-walled houses were refaced with brick.

From the 18th century onwards, as good building timber became scarcer, wooden-frame houses were more often than not completely rendered over. There is a modern tendency to expose these timbers, but they were never meant to be seen.

If the house walls are less than a foot thick, there is probably a timber frame beneath; thicker walls, tapering from the base, and rounded corners indicate a clay construction. The windows also tend to be smaller. Many clay buildings are fairly recent, from the late 18th or early 19th centuries when there was a demand for cheap construction.

Dating clay houses can be difficult and the best clues come from architectural features, but the material used for the base of the wall may help: stone or flint was used earlier, brick later.

The rendering of timber-frame houses became popular in the 16th and 17th centuries (even in good quality housing in East Anglia) with lime plaster laid on laths. While often plain (and white- or colour-washed), the plaster could be scribed or moulded into intricate designs, known as pargetting. This can be seen from the late 16th century and was at its height in the late 17th and early 18th centuries, but plain plastering was in vogue again in the mid-18th century. Pargetting enjoyed another comeback in the late 19th century.

Stucco, a cement-like plaster, was widely used by Georgian and early Victorian builders, especially in towns.

For more details turn to pages 200 to 201.

Timber-Framed Houses: what to look out for

Large panel framing: 14th/15th to 16th century

The earliest form of framing, found in all areas by the mid-15th century. Only generally found in less important houses after the beginning of the 16th century; uncommon after the mid-16th.

Plain large panel: 14th and 15th centuries

Arch-bracing: 14th century onwards, common in Midlands.

Tension-bracing: 15th century onwards, popular in the south-east

191

Smaller panel framing: 15th/16th to 17th century

Seen in larger houses in the north and west from the mid-15th century. Much later in other areas and generally in smaller houses. Widespread in smaller houses by the late 16th and 17th centuries.

Plain small framing: mid-15th century onwards. Note small angle-brace.

Close studding: late 15th to 17th century

Most popular in the south-east and often associated with jettying. Panel members are same thickness as studs. They become more widely spaced as time went on. A middle rail may sometimes be seen in most areas except the north-east. Note: small framing and close studding use a lot of timber and were used on show elevations (rather like jettying) so large panels are frequently used at back or sides of house.

Close-studding: Late 15th century onwards.

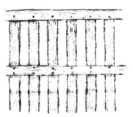

Rough-timbered light hardwood framing: late 17th to mid-18th century

Seen from the late 17th century onwards as good timber becomes scarce. Not to be confused with 18th and 19th century studwork (see below). Often plastered over, the plaster sometimes moulded and decorated, especially in East Anglia. (See Rendering: pargetting)

Rough timber, light framing, seen from the 17th century onwards

Softwood light stud framing: 18th and 19th centuries

Generally rendered on laths, weatherboarded or tiled over and not intended to be seen (although sometimes exposed in restoration). Sometimes exposed brick panels and studs, the timbers and brickwork equally important structurally, unlike earlier timber-framing. Timber frame building died out by the 19th century, except for farm buildings, outhouses and industrial buildings.

Jettying: 15th to early 17th century

Seen in the 15th century Wealden houses and common in Tudor town houses. It spread to the countryside and the village, but by the mid-17th century was largely confined to towns and the West Midlands.

Timber-frame infilling

The earliest infilling was wattle and daub, finished with limewash which sometimes continued over timbers. Timbers were generally not darkened, except in the north and west, especially in later ornamental work. (Blackening timbers developed in the 19th century.) By the 16th century in the south and east, brick comes in, sometimes in a herring-bone pattern. Brick infill gradually spread to other areas.

Typical examples of timber-framed house styles

Cruck house: 14th to 18th century. See text page 13 for details.

Wealden house: 15th and 16th century. See text page 16 for details.

Jettied house: 15th to early 17th century.
See text page 26 for details.

For further clues on dating, turn to Architectural Details, pp 202 to 205.

Stone-Built Houses: what to look out for

Stone building techniques: can all be used in different periods, check architectural details for dating.

Random rubble.

Coursed random rubble with larger, more regular stone quoins.

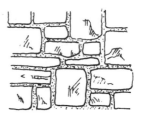

Flint with brick lacing course and quoins.

Fine ashlar masonry, typical of Georgian period. (Watch for rendered imitations.)

Typical examples of stone-built houses

Rubble stone laithe house: 18th century. See text page 71 for details.

Cotswold stone house: 17th to 19th centuries. See text page 67 for details.

Georgian house: 18th century. See text page 32 for details.

For further clues on dating, turn to Architectural Details, pp 202 to 205.

Brick-Built Houses: what to look out for

Brick sizes

Early bricks of around the 14th and 15th centuries are about 2 inches high and 12 by 6 inches across. Brick thickness was fixed in 1571 at 2¼ inches high and 9 by 4½ inches across. These were called Statute bricks. Thick bricks found during the Brick Tax period (late 18th to mid-19th centuries) are 3 inches high and more. Modern bricks are usually 2½ inches high (more in the north).

Brick colours

Red brick was popular in the 16th, 17th and early 18th centuries. Grey and brown was increasingly used in the 18th, with red brick dressings at quoins, door and window openings. By the late 18th century red was considered too bright: grey, yellow (London 'stock') and East Anglian 'whites' (pale grey) were widely used. By the late 19th century 'stock' had acquired a working class image, red made a comeback in better class houses.

Brick patterns (bonds)

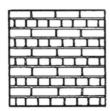

English bond, typical of 16th and 17th centuries.

Flemish bond: common in 17th century, largely replaces English bond by early 18th.

Header bond: popular in the 18th century.

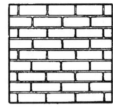

Stretcher bond: generally seen in modern cavity walling.

Typical examples of brick-built house styles.

16th to 17th century brick house. See text page 24 for details.

Queen Anne House: late 17th early 18th centuries. See text page 29 for details.

Victorian terrace house: 19th century. See text page 46 for details.

For further clues on dating, turn to Architectural Details pp 202 to 205.

Rendered Houses: what to look out for

Plaster laid on horizontal laths.

Pargetting: generally late 16th to middle 18th century.

Typical examples of clay-built or rendered houses

Cob cottage, typical of Devon: medieval to 19th century. See text page 59 for details.

Rendered timber house with pargetting, late 16th to middle 18th century. See text page 25 for details.

Georgian: 18th to early 19th centuries. See text page 33 for details.

For further clues on dating, turn to Architectural Details pp 202 to 205.

201

Architectural Details

Architectural details like the shape, size and style of windows and doors, and their surrounds, can also give further clues to the dating of the house. But it is important to remember that such features may well have been altered or replaced over the years and their evidence must be weighed with other signs, like the shape of the house and the materials used in its construction.

The Windows

Early windows tended to be long and low. In the smaller medieval and early Tudor houses, they were usually unglazed and had internal shutters. The window space was divided by upright timber (or stone) mullions. The design of these mullions changed over the years and can give clues to dating. By the mid-16th century, glazing was more widespread and the mullions were adapted accordingly. By the late 16th and early 17th centuries side-hung casements, usually with iron frames, had become more common and in the 18th century timber became more common for casement windows. Such windows often replaced the old mullioned ones in the smaller house and cottage.

By the 17th century as the influence of classical designs spread to everyday houses, windows in the better ones became taller and narrower, often only two lights wide and divided with a horizontal transom as well as a vertical mullion, the 'cross casement' window. By the 18th century the diamond pattern of the leaded lights gave way to a rectangular one. Brick houses of the 17th and early 18th centuries often had contrasting window surrounds and exaggerated keystones.

Sash windows came in during the late 17th and early 18th centuries. Early sash frames were flush with the wall but, because of the fire hazard, London Building Acts in 1707 and 1709 required them to be set back four inches. This change gradually spread to most of the rest of the country. A 1774 Act also required the frames to be recessed behind reveals, so little of the frame is visible from the outside. Glazing bars became lighter as time progressed and could be very thin indeed by the 19th century.

Window taxes from 1695 to the end of the 18th century explain why some windows are blocked up, but 'blind' windows were often deliberately inserted in 18th century designs to obtain symmetry. Genuine brick tax blockings are usually obvious with the brick flush with and a different colour from the surrounding walling.

By the 19th century larger panes of glass were available and glazing bars could be omitted or removed (which often spoiled the appearance of older windows).

Window shapes:

A 13th century medieval window with Geometric tracery. The medieval influence was strong in the Gothic revival of the 19th century.

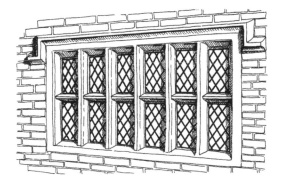

A mullioned and transomed Tudor window with a hood mould.

A Georgian sash window, showing classical influence.

For more information on windows see pp 118 to 130.

The Doors

Medieval and Tudor doors tended to have pointed arched heads, but these arches became flatter as time progressed. At first (in the 14th and 15th centuries) the two-centred arch was popular; the four-centred arch appeared in the 15th century and continued until the 17th, becoming flatter. Other variations included the ogee and the shouldered arch.

The vertical plank doors were more often than not hung directly on to the wall, with a metal strap slotting on to a vertical pin. If there was a door frame it would be heavily timbered.

By the end of the 17th century, the classical influence was becoming apparent even in smaller houses, and square-headed doorways became the norm. Flat door hoods supported by console brackets characterised early 18th century doors while the latter part of the century saw the development of the classical pediment (with ornate variations) above moulded pilasters or modillion brackets. Lighter panelled doors were common by the 18th century and the lighter doors could be hung on concealed butt hinges.

The London Building Acts of the late 18th century discouraged the use of projecting timberwork which was replaced in the capital, and later elsewhere, by a more ornate treatment of brick and stone surrounds, although throughout the 18th and 19th centuries many everyday houses stuck with simple square-headed doors.

Fanlights were another development seen in Queen Anne and Georgian times, while the end of the 18th century saw the increasing use of open ornamental cast iron porches, often added to older homes. Stone, or mock stone, porches with classical columns were common in late 18th and early 19th century terraced town houses.

A note of caution on relying too much on door styles for dating: since the door is a focus of attention as well as in constant use, owners often upgraded it using the current styles and the house may in fact be much older.

Door styles:

A 15th century plank and ledge door.

An 18th century Georgian classical style door.

A mid Victorian door.

For more information on door styles see pp 131 to 139.

Local Records for
Dating Houses

To pin-point accurately the date of a particular house, local records can be very useful. It can also be fun to discover who has lived in a particular house. The starting point for searching for information is the local Record Office relating to the site of the house. There are County Record Offices, of course, but there are now also district or borough record offices, such as those for the Metropolitan Boroughs around Manchester or Birmingham.

County and other record offices hold much of the material needed for detailed inquiries of this kind. Most central libraries will also have a local history or local studies collection: Manchester Central Library or Aylesbury Reference Library are examples. This type of collection usually includes copies of local parish registers, old maps and census returns on microfilm, so the following notes can equally relate to County Record Offices or reference library local studies collections.

The most useful documents include:

Ordnance Survey Maps
These can position the house exactly and it is possible to tell if the house has been renumbered or the street renamed since it was built. Most collections will include old large-scale Ordnance Survey maps which should allow you to see your house and its surroundings over a century ago.

Tithe Maps
When church tithes were changed to an annual charge in 1840, a map was produced showing the divisions of parish land in numbered portions. The numbers relate to an accompanying Tithe Apportionment which lists the amount of land allotted to these numbers together with information about the owners and their status. Usually the maps are highly accurate and the whole document gives a splendid snapshot of the community around your house over a century and a half ago.

Rate Books

Most County Record Offices keep a card index showing when areas were first rated. By diligent searching it may be possible to determine when a property was first built and who has lived in it since.

Other valuable sources of information usually kept by County Record Offices include:

Electoral Registers
Census Returns
Street Directories
Land Tax Returns
Estate Records
Borough Records

Census Returns are particularly interesting for, taken at ten year intervals, they give every occupant of a house and of the whole community from 1841 to 1891. In 2001 the next census, for 1901, will become available for public use.

The majority of County Record Offices also keep a card index of properties (usually middle class dwellings and above) which detail anything known about them. Many keep a list of the names of people featured in documents in their possession such as wills and leases.

The archivist at the County Record Office is the best person to advise on how to get the most out of the wealth of information held there. Other helpful sources of information include local history societies and local museums.

The Council's Conservation Officer can also give advice on dating your house and, if it is listed, can show you the list description. These statutory lists usually include an expert's assessment of the date of a building, either based on documents or definite information or on a visual assessment. These estimates of age are usually accurate and you can also see the list for your area at a major public library.

Glossary

ashlar	Smoothly cut blocks of stone with fine joints.
Baroque	Late 17th and early 18th century style using exaggeratedly large classical elements including columns, a dramatic use of spaces and mass e.g. Blenheim Palace, Oxfordshire.
bressumer	A main horizontal rail or timber in a timber-framed building, often between storeys.
buttery	Domestic beer, wine and 'wet' goods store from *boutellerie* or 'butt' (barrel) and bottle store.
came	'H' section strips of lead to hold pieces of glass in leaded lights.
capital	A carved block at the top of a column or pier.
casement	A window hinged at the side.
cob	Walls made from earth or clay mixed with straw.
collar	A beam connecting a pair of rafters between the tie beam and apex.
cornice	A moulded projection at the top of a wall, classical in style.
crown post	A post rising from the centre of a tie beam to the collar beam in a roof truss.
cruck	Pairs of large timbers rising from the ground to the apex of a roof.
double pile	A house two rooms deep in plan.
dragon beam	A diagonal floor beam running to the corner of a building jettied on both sides, often carved with a dragon's head at the end.
entablature	The lintel area with cornice and fascia above classical columns.
galletting	Small chips of dark stone pressed into mortar joints, common in the Greensand areas of Kent, Surrey, Sussex and Hampshire.
hall house	Medieval house plan based on a large room or hall open to the roof.

header brick	A brick laid endways with its short face exposed.
jetty	In timber-framed construction, projecting or over-sailing upper floors.
king post	A post rising from the centre of the tie beam to the apex of the roof.
laithe house	A house with a barn, cow house or stables in range and often sharing the same roof. Found in Yorkshire and the North of England.
lobby entry plan	A house plan from the late 16th to early 18th century in which an entrance lobby is formed in front of an axial stack, usually with back-to-back fireplaces. Often with a stair tucked in behind the stack.
longhouse	A West Country and North-Western house plan in which the occupants and the cattle and beasts share the same entrance, one turning into the house part, the beasts into the byre.
mathematical tiles	Hanging tiles with brick-shaped lower parts which combine to look like solid brickwork. Found in Surrey, Sussex, Kent, Wiltshire and occasionally elsewhere.
mortice	A slot let into a beam for a tenon to fit.
mullion	A vertical division in a window.
outshot	A lean-to attachment, usually contained within a continuation downwards of the main roof.
Palladian	Sixteenth century Venetian Renaissance style of Andrea Palladio introduced into England by Inigo Jones and revived in the early Georgian period. Characterised by elegant classical proportions, stucco, columns and pediments.
pantry	The dry goods store in a house, from the French word *paneterie*, bread store.
pargetting	Ornamental plastering of outside walls, in panels or relief, and a notable characteristic of East Anglia and Essex.
pediment	A low-pitched triangular gable of classical design, usually surmounting columns or pilasters.
pilaster	A shallow projecting square column with base and capitals in classically derived architecture.
purlin	A beam running the length of a roof, either supported by a collar in the centre or along each side supported by the principal rafters.

209

queen post	Vertical posts rising from the outer thirds of a tie beam to support the purlins or ends of a collar beam.
rubble	Stone walling where the stone is roughly finished and shaped.
sash	A window unit that normally slides up and down or, less commonly, sideways.
solar	An upper living room, literally the *solarium* or sun room. Normally the private chamber for the owner of a hall house.
stretcher brick	Brick laid lengthways.
stucco	Render with ground stone content, but more commonly any white or white-painted render.
tenon	A projecting timber tongue that fits into a mortice to join two timbers. Usually fixed with an oak peg.
tie beam	A cross beam tying the feet of a pair of rafters to stop the roof spreading.
voussoir	One of the wedge-shaped stones that form an arch.
Wealden house	In hall and crosswing timber-framed houses a type where there is a single roof carried past the recessed central hall bays on brackets.

Bibliography

AISLED TIMBER HALLS AND RELATED BUILDINGS, *Cecil Hewitt*, Transactions of the Ancient Monuments Society, 1976

BRITISH HISTORICAL ROOF-TYPES AND THEIR MEMBERS: A CLASSIFICATION, *R. A. Cordingly*, Transactions of the Ancient Monuments Society, 1961

THE BUILDINGS OF ENGLAND, *Nikolaus Pevsner & Others*, Penguin, 1951 to date (A monumental achievement with a volume(s) for each English County, many now in their second editions)

THE BUILDINGS OF BRITAIN, *ed.Alistair Service*, 4 volumes, Barrie and Jenkins, 1982

BUILDING STONES OF ENGLAND AND WALES, *Norman Davey*, Standing Conference for Local History, 1976

CARE FOR OLD HOUSES, *Pamela Cunnington*, A & C Black, 1991

THE CARE OF OLD BUILDINGS TODAY, *Donald Insall*, Architectural Press, 1972

CHIMNEYS IN OLD BUILDINGS, *G. B. A. Williams*, S.P.A.B., 1976

DISCOVERING TIMBER-FRAMED BUILDINGS, *Richard Harris*, Shire, 1978

ENGLISH COTTAGES AND SMALL FARMHOUSES, *Paul Oliver*, Arts Council, 1975

THE ENGLISH COUNTRY COTTAGE, *R. J. Brown*, Robert Hale, 1979

THE ENGLISH FARMHOUSE AND COTTAGE, *Maurice Barley*, Routledge and Kegan Paul, 1961

THE ENGLISH HOME, *H. E. Priestley*, Muller, 1971

THE FAMILY HOUSE IN ENGLAND, *Andrew Henderson*, Phoenix House, 1964

GEORGIAN HOUSES FOR ALL, *John Woodforde*, Routledge and Kegan Paul, 1978

GUIDE TO WESTERN ARCHITECTURE, *John Gloag*, George Allen and Unwin, 1958

THE HOUSE AND COTTAGE HANDBOOK, *Neville Whittaker*, Civic Trust for North East, 1976

HOW OLD IS YOUR HOUSE?, *Pamela Cunnington*, Alpha Books, 1980

THE IDEA OF THE VILLAGE, *Gillian Darley*, Arts Council, 1976

ILLUSTRATED HANDBOOK OF VERNACULAR ARCHITECTURE, *Ron Brunskill*, Faber, 1978

LONDON: THE ART OF GEORGIAN BUILDING, *Dan Cruikshank and Peter Wyld*, The Architectural Press, 1975

THE MAKING OF THE ENGLISH LANDSCAPE, *W.G.Hoskins*, Penguin, 1970

MEDIEVAL ENGLAND, *Colin Platt*, Routledge and Kegan Paul, 1978

OLD ENGLISH HOUSES, *Hugh Braun*, Faber, 1962

ON THE DATING OF ENGLISH HOUSES FROM EXTERNAL EVIDENCE, *J. T. Smith and E. M Yates*, Field Studies, 1968

AN OUTLINE OF EUROPEAN ARCHITECTURE, *Nikolaus Pevsner*, Penguin, (revised 1968)

THE PATTERN OF ENGLISH BUILDING, *Alec Clifton-Taylor*, Faber, 1972

PICTORIAL HISTORY OF ENGLISH ARCHITECTURE, *John Betjeman*, John Murray, 1972

THE SHELL BOOK OF COTTAGES, *Richard Reid*, Michael Joseph, 1977

THE SMALLER ENGLISH HOUSE, *Lyndon Cave*, Hale, 1981

THE STORY OF WESTERN ARCHITECTURE, *Bill Risebero*, Herbert Press, 1979

STRENGTHENING TIMBER FLOORS, *John MacGregor*, S.P.A.B., 1973

TIMBER FRAMED BUILDINGS, *Richard Harris*, Arts Council, 1980

TRADITIONAL BUILDINGS ACCESSIBLE TO THE PUBLIC, *J.R.Armstrong*, EP Publishing, 1979

TRADITIONAL BUILDINGS OF BRITAIN, *Ron Brunskill*, Victor Gollancz, 1981

TRADITIONAL BUILDINGS OF ENGLAND, *Anthony Quiney*, Thames & Hudson, 1990

UNDERSTANDING TOWNS, *David Stenhouse*, Wayland, 1977

THE VILLAGE GREEN, *Paul Oliver*, Arts Council

YOUR COUNTRY COTTAGE, *Robert Edmunds*, David and Charles, 1970

YOUR HOUSE: THE OUTSIDE VIEW, *John Prizeman*, Hutchinson, 1975

INDEX